Influential Boxing Legends of All Time: Ezzard Charles

Elizabeth Dummel

The role of the book within our culture is changing. The change is brought on by new ways to acquire & use content, the rapid dissemination of information and real-time peer collaboration on a global scale. Despite these changes one thing is clear--"the book" in it's traditional form continues to play an important role in learning and communication. The book you are holding in your hands utilizes the unique characteristics of the Internet -- relying on web infrastructure and collaborative tools to share and use resources in keeping with the characteristics of the medium (user-created, defying control, etc.)--while maintaining all the convenience and utility of a real book.

Contents

Articles

Personal life   **87**

Cultural Impact   **157**

References

Introduction

Ezzard Charles

Statistics	
Real name	Ezzard Mack Charles
Nickname(s)	Cincinnati Cobra
Rated at	Heavyweight Light Heavyweight
Height	6 ft 0 in (1.83 m)
Reach	73 in (185 cm)
Nationality	American
Birth date	July 7, 1921
Birth place	Lawrenceville, Georgia
Death date	May 28, 1975 (aged 53)
Death place	Chicago, Illinois
Stance	Orthodox
Boxing record	
Total fights	119
Wins	93
Wins by KO	52
Losses	25
Draws	1

No contests	0

Ezzard Mack Charles (July 7, 1921 − May 28, 1975) was an African-American professional boxer and former world heavyweight champion. He holds wins over numerous Hall of Fame fighters in three different weight classes. Charles retired with a record of 93 wins, 25 losses and 1 draw.

Career

He was born in Lawrenceville, Georgia, but is commonly thought of as a Cincinnatian. Charles graduated from Woodward High School in Cincinnati where he was already becoming a well-known fighter. Known as "The Cincinnati Cobra," Charles is best remembered for his wins as a heavyweight, but most experts feelWikipedia:Avoid weasel words he was in his prime as a light heavyweight. Although he never won the championship at that weight, Ring magazine has rated him as the greatest light heavyweight of all time.

Ezzard Charles started his career as a featherweight in the amateurs, where he had a record of 42-0. In 1938, he won the Diamond Belt Middleweight Champion. He followed this up in 1939 by winning the Chicago Golden Gloves tournament of champions. He won the national AAU Middleweight Championship in 1939. He turned pro in 1940, knocking out Melody Johnson in the 4th round. Charles won all of his first 15 fights before being defeated by veteran Ken Overlin. Victories over future Hall of Famers Teddy Yarosz and the much avoided Charley Burley had started to solidify Charles as a top contender in the Middleweight division. However, he served in the U.S. military during World War II and was unable to fight professionally in 1945.

He returned to boxing after the war as a light heavyweight, picking up many notable wins over leading light heavyweight as well as heavyweight contenders Archie Moore, Jimmy Bivins, Lloyd Marshall, and Elmer Ray. Shortly after his knock-out of Moore in their third and final meeting, tragedy struck. Charles fought a young contender named Sam Baroudi, knocking him out in Round 10. Baroudi died of the injuries he sustained in this bout. Charles was so devastated he almost gave up fighting. Charles was unable to secure a title shot at light heavyweight, and moved up to heavyweight. After knocking out Joe Baksi and Johnny Haynes, Charles won the vacant National Boxing Association world heavyweight title when he outpointed Jersey Joe Walcott over 15 rounds on June 22, 1949. The following year, he outpointed his idol and former world heavyweight champion Joe Louis to become the recognized lineal champion. Successful defenses against Walcott, Lee Oma and Joey Maxim would follow.

In 1951, Charles fought Walcott a third time and lost the title by knockout in the seventh round. Charles lost a controversial decision in the fourth and final bout. If Charles had won this fight he would have become the first man in history to regain the heavyweight championship. Remaining a top contender with wins over Rex Layne, Tommy Harrison, and Coley Wallace, Charles knocked out Bob Satterfield in an eliminator bout for the right to challenge Heavyweight Champion Rocky Marciano.

His two stirring battles with Marciano are regarded as ring classics. In the first bout, held in June 1954, he valiantly took Rocky the distance, going down on points in a vintage heavyweight bout. Charles is the only man ever to last the full 15-round distance against Marciano. In their September rematch, a severely cut Marciano rallied to KO Charles in the 8th round, in a bout that was named Ring Magazine's "Fight of the Year." Financial problems forced Charles to continue fighting, losing 12 of his final 23 fights. He retired with a record of 96-25-1 (58 KOs).

Charles was also a respected double bass player who played with some of the jazz greats in the 40s and 50s at such notable places as Birdland. He was very close with Rocky Marciano and a neighbor and friend of Muhammed Ali when they both lived on 85th street in Chicago. Charles also starred in one motion picture: "Mau Mau Drums", an independent (and unreleased) jungle-adventure film shot in and around Cincinnati in 1960 by filmmaker Earl Schwieterman.

Death

Ezzard Charles died May 28, 1975, in Chicago from amyotrophic lateral sclerosis (ALS) also known as Lou Gehrig's Disease, aged 53, and was interred in the historic Burr Oak Cemetery, in Alsip, Illinois. In 1976 Cincinnati honored Charles by changing the name of Lincoln Park Drive to Ezzard Charles Drive. This was the street of his residence during the height of his career.

He was elected to the International Boxing Hall of Fame in 1990.

In 2002, Charles was ranked #13 on Ring Magazine's list of the 80 Best Fighters of the Last 80 Years.

Recognition

In 2006, Ezzard Charles was named the 11th greatest fighter of all time by the IBRO (International Boxing Research Organisation).

> The "Cincinnati Cobra" was a master boxer of extraordinary skill and ability. He had speed, agility, fast hands and excellent footwork. Charles possessed a masterful jab and was a superb combination puncher. He was at his peak as a light-heavyweight. His record is quite impressive. Against top rate opposition like Archie Moore, Charley Burley, Lloyd Marshall, Jimmy Bivins, and Joey Maxim he was an impressive 16-2 combined. Despite being a natural light-heavy he won the heavyweight title and made 9 successful title defenses. Nearly 25% of voters had Charles in the top 10. Half of the voters had him in the top 15. Two thirds of voters had him inside the top 20.

ESPN online ranks Ezzard Charles as the 27th greatest boxer of all time, ahead of such notable fighters as Mike Tyson, Bernard Hopkins, Floyd Mayweather Jr., Larry Holmes and Jake LaMotta.

In 2009, Boxing Magazine listed Ezzard Charles as the greatest Light Heavyweight fighter ever, beating the likes of Archie Moore, Bob Foster, Gene Tunney.

Prominent Boxing historian, Bert Sugar, listed Charles as the 7th greatest Heavyweight of all time.

See also

- List of heavyweight boxing champions

Further reading

- Grace, Kevin & Grace, Joshua (2006). *Cincinnati Boxing*. Chicago: Arcadia. ISBN 0738541125.

External links

- Professional boxing record for Ezzard Charles [1] from BoxRec
- Ezzard Charles [2] at Find a Grave

Professional Career

Ken Overlin

Ken Overlin (August 15, 1910 - July 24, 1969), was an American-born middleweight boxer who fought professionally from 1931 to 1944, compiling a record of 131 wins (23 by knockout), 18 losses, and 9 draws.

Overlin began boxing in the navy, having many of his early bouts in cities where his ship the *U.S.S. Tennessee* was stationed. Overlin would do most of his work based out of Norfolk, Virginia and in cities along the American eastern seaboard. A middleweight contender by the mid-to-late 1930s, Overlin received his first title shot on September 11, 1937 when he was knocked out in the 4th round of a match with Freddie Steele in Seattle. Overlin would win recognition as a world middleweight champion by the New York State Athletic Commission on May 23, 1940, when he won a unanimous decision over Ceferino Garcia at Madison Square Garden. Overlin would successfully defend his title twice against Steve Belloise, before losing his title to Billy Soose on May 9, 1941. Overlin would continue fighting without defeat until 1945, scoring notable wins over Ezzard Charles and Al Hostak, before his retirement.

External links

- Professional boxing record for Ken Overlin [1] from BoxRec

Teddy Yarosz

Teddy Yarosz (24 June 1910 – 29 March 1974) was an American athlete in boxing. He held the world middleweight boxing championship during 1934-1935.

Personal life

Yarosz was born in Pittsburgh, Pennsylvania. His brother Tommy Yarosz also became a boxer.

Professional boxing career

Yarosz became a professional boxer in 1929, trained by Ray Arcel. He won the NYSAC World Middleweight Title and National Boxing Association World Middleweight Title with a win over Vince Dundee in 1934. He lost the belt to Babe Risko in 1935.

Yarosz was featured on the cover of the January 1934 issue of The Ring magazine.

Yarosz was inducted into the International Boxing Hall of Fame in the Class of 2006.

References

- Professional boxing record for Teddy Yarosz [1] from BoxRec

Charley Burley

Statistics	
Real name	Charles Duane Burley
Rated at	Middleweight
Nationality	American
Birth date	September 6, 1917
Birth place	Bessemer, Pennsylvania
Death date	October 16, 1992 (aged 75)
Stance	Orthodox
Boxing record	
Total fights	98
Wins	83
Wins by KO	50
Losses	12
Draws	2
No contests	1

Charley Burley (September 6, 1917 – October 16, 1992) was a boxer of the 1940s, compiling a record of 83 wins (50 by knockout), 12 losses, and 2 draws with 1 "no contest". However, because he was so formidable, Burley was never granted a title shot by any of the welterweight and middleweight champions of that era and was also avoided by many of the top white contenders (Burley's father was black and his mother white). Among the fighters who "ducked" Burley were Hall of Famers Billy Conn (who fought Joe Louis for the heavyweight title), Frenchman Marcel Cerdan (who was supposed to face Burley in his American debut), Jake LaMotta (who had fought the likes of powerpuncher Bob Satterfield, Sugar Ray Robinson, and Holman Williams, who was Burley's greatest rival), and even Sugar Ray Robinson, considered by many boxing historians as the best pound-for-pound fighter of all time.

Of course, not everyone ducked the slick Pittsburgh warrior. Burley won two out of three matches against future welterweight champion Fritzie Zivic, defeated the great Archie Moore by decision, and easily defeated future NYSAC middleweight king Billy Soose. Burley also faced future heavyweight champion Ezzard Charles, but dropped two 10 round decisions to him (the bouts were contested within a five week period, sandwiching a fight against Williams). Another notable Burley fight was the one against heavyweight J.D. Turner, who outweighed him by around 70 lbs. "Turner, face beaten to raw beefsteak in six rounds, failed to answer the bell for the seventh." (The Ring, June 1942). Burley himself was never stopped in 98 bouts.

There exists only one near complete film of Burley in action: his second fight with Oakland Billy Smith in 1946. It shows a conservative counter-puncher taming a much larger opponent with relative ease.

Burley's former sparring partner A.J. "Blackie" Nelson offers this comparison: "I see a lot of Charley in this kid, Roy Jones Junior. Both had unorthodox styles, could hit you from any angle, both hard to hit. Charley jabbed more than Jones, if Jones would concentrate on boxing as Charley did, he would become an all-time great."

Eddie Futch, the great trainer, called Burley "the finest all-around fighter I ever saw."

Burley was named to the Ring Magazine's list of 100 greatest punchers of all time, elected to the Boxing Hall of Fame in 1983 and the International Boxing Hall of Fame in 1992.

Burley was ranked 39th on Ring Magazine's list of the 80 Best Fighters of the Last 80 Years.

An exhibit at The Western Pennsylvania Sports Museum at the Pittsburgh History Center states that Burley was the model for the character Troy in August Wilson's play Fences.

See also

- List of bare-knuckle boxers
- Pro Record [1]

Archie Moore

Statistics	
Real name	Archibald Wright
Nickname(s)	The Old Mongoose
Rated at	Heavyweight
Height	5 ft 11 in (1.80 m)
Reach	75 in (191 cm)
Nationality	American
Birth date	December 13, 1913
Birth place	Benoit, Mississippi
Death date	December 9, 1998 (aged 84)
Death place	San Diego, California
Stance	Orthodox
Boxing record	
Total fights	220 (1 no-decision)
Wins	185
Wins by KO	131* (* Varied figures)
Losses	23
Draws	11

Archie Moore, born Archibald Wright (December 13, 1913 – December 9, 1998), was light heavyweight world boxing champion (1952–1959 and 1961) who had one of the longest professional careers in the history of that sport. Nicknamed "The Old Mongoose", Moore holds the record for the most career knockouts (131). He ranks #4 on *Ring Magazine's* list of *100 greatest punchers of all time*, and is rated by prominent boxing website BoxRec as the greatest pound-for-pound boxer of all time.

A native of Benoit, Mississippi, Moore was raised in St. Louis, Mo.. An important figure in the American black community, he became involved in African American causes once his days as a fighter were over. He also established himself as a successful character actor in television and film. Moore died in his adopted home of San Diego, California.

Before boxing

Moore often found himself in trouble as a youngster, and was in a reformatory until 1934. In 1935, he began his boxing career with nine fights as a boxer, winning 5 and losing 4. (He also claimed to have boxed under the name "Fourth of July Kid," so he may have had even more fights.)

Professional boxing career

He turned professional in 1938 and boxed all but one of his 12 bouts that year in San Diego. Moore had eight bouts in 1939, going 5-2 during that span, with one "no contest". He lost to former middleweight champion and future Hall of Famer Teddy Yarosz during that time, and his no contest was against Jack Coggins, in eight rounds. In 1940, Moore a tour of Australia had him fighting in Melbourne, Tasmania, Adelaide and Sydney. He won all of his seven bouts there, including six by knockout. Upon returning to the United States, he defeated Pancho Ramirez by a knockout in five, but lost to Shorty Hogue on a six round decision.

First retirement and comeback

Moore had four fights in 1941, during which he went 2-1-1, with the draw against Eddie Booker. By then, however, he had suffered through several stomach ulcers, with the resulting operations, and he announced his retirement from boxing.

His retirement was brief, however, and by 1942 he was back in the ring. He won his first six bouts that year, including a second round knockout of Hogue in a rematch, and a ten round decision over Jack Chase. He met Booker in a rematch, and reached the same conclusion as their first meeting had: another 10 round draw.

In 1943, Moore fought seven bouts, winning five and losing two. He won and then lost the California State Middleweight title against Chase, both by 15 round decisions, and beat Chase again in his last bout of that year, in a ten round decision. He also lost a decision to Aaron Wade that year.

The Atlantic coast

In 1944, he had nine bouts, going 7-2. His last bout that year marked his debut on the Atlantic Coast, and the level of his opposition began to improve. He beat Jimmy Hayden by a knockout in five, lost to future Hall of Famer Charlie Burley by a decision, and to Booker by a knockout in eight.

He won his first eight bouts of 1945, impressing Atlantic coast boxing experts, and earning a fight with future IBHOF enshrinee Jimmy Bivins, who defeated Moore by a knockout in six at Cleveland. He returned to the Eastern Seaboard to fight five more times before that year was over. He met, among others, future IBHOF enshrinee Holman Williams during that span, losing a ten round decision, and knocking him out in eleven in the rematch.

By 1946, Moore had moved to the light heavyweight division, and he went 5-2-1 that year, beating contender Curtis Sheppard, but losing to future world heavyweight champion and Hall of Famer Ezzard Charles by a decision in ten, and drawing with old nemesis Chase. By then, Moore began complaining publicly that, according to him, none of boxing's world champions would risk their titles fighting him.

1947 was essentially a year of rematches for Moore. He went 7-1 that year, his one loss being to Charles. He beat Chase by a knockout in nine, Sheppard by a decision in ten and Bivins by a knockout in nine. He also defeated Burt Lytell, by a decision in ten.

He fought a solid 14 fights in 1948, losing again to Charles by a knockout in nine, losing to Leonard Morrow by a knockout in the first, to Henry Hall by a decision in ten and to Lloyd Gibson by a disqualification in four. But he also beat Ted Lowry, by a decision in ten, and Hall in a rematch, also by decision.

1949 was also a good year for Moore: He had 13 bouts that year, going 12-1. He defeated the *Alabama Kid* twice; by knockout in four and by knockout in three, Bob Satterfield by a knockout in three, Bivins by a knockout in eight, future world Light Heavyweight champion and IBHOF inductee Harold Johnson by a decision, Bob Sikes by a knockout in three, and Phil Muscato by a decision. He lost to Clinton Bacon by a disqualification in six.

By Moore's standards, 1950 was a vacation year for him: he only had two fights, winning both, including a 10 round decision in a rematch with Lydell.

In 1951, Moore boxed 18 times, winning 16, losing one, and drawing one. He went on an Argentinian tour, fighting seven times there, winning six and drawing one. In between those seven fights, he found time for a trip to Montevideo, Uruguay, where he defeated Vicente Quiroz by a knockout in six. He knocked out Bivins in nine, and split two decisions with Johnson.

World Light Heavyweight Champion

1952 was one of the most important years in Moore's life. After beating Johnson, heavyweight contenders Jimmy Slade, Bob Dunlap, and Clarence Henry and light heavyweight Clinton Bacon (knocked out in four in a rematch), Moore was finally given an opportunity at age thirty-nine to fight for the title of world light heavyweight champion and future IBHOF honoree Joey Maxim.

Maxim had just defeated the great Sugar Ray Robinson by a technical knockout in 14 rounds, forcing Robinson to quit in his corner due to heat exhaustion. Against Maxim, Moore consistently landed powerful right hands, hurting him several times en route to a fifteen round decision. After sixteen long years he had finally achieved his dream.

He was far from done, however. The next year, Moore won all nine of his bouts, including a 10 round non title win against then fringe heavyweight contender Nino Valdez of Cuba, and a 15 round decision over Maxim in a rematch to retain the belt. He made two more bouts in Argentina before the end of the year.

In 1954, he had only four fights, retaining the title in a third fight with Maxim, who once again went the 15 round distance, and versus Johnson, who he knocked out in 14. He also beat highly ranked heavyweight Bob Baker.

In 1955, Moore again beat Valdez, who by that time was the no. 1 heavyweight contender, and defended against Bobo Olson, the world middleweight champion and future Hall of Famer who was coming off a decision victory over Joey Maxim, by a knockout in three.

On September 21, 1955, Moore went up in weight to face future Hall of Famer Rocky Marciano for Marciano's heavyweight championship. Moore briefly dropped Marciano in the second round (the second and last time Marciano had ever been knocked down), but Marciano recovered and knocked Moore down five times, knocking him out in the ninth to retain the belt. It was Marciano's sixth and last title defense before retiring in 1956.

In 1956, Moore fought mostly as a heavyweight but did retain his light heavyweight title with a ten round knockout over Yolande Pompey in London. He won 11 bouts in a row before challenging again for the world heavyweight crown. The title was left vacant by Marciano, but Moore lost to Floyd Patterson by a knockout in five. (Patterson, yet another future Hall of Famer, himself made history that night, becoming, at the age of 21, the youngest world heavyweight champion yet, a record he would hold until 1986.)

Moore won all six of his bouts during 1957. Among those wins was an easy 10-round decision over heavyweight contender Hans Kalbfell in Germany, a KO-7 over highly ranked Tony Anthony to retain the light heavyweight title, a one-sided 10-round decision over light heavyweight contender Eddie Cotton in a non-title bout, and a 4th round knockout of future top ten heavyweight contender Roger Rischer.

In 1958, Moore had 10 fights, going 9-0-1 during that span. His fight with Yvon Durelle in particular was of note: defending his world light heavyweight title in Montreal, he was felled three times in round one, and once again in round five, but then dropped Durelle in round 10 and won by a knockout in the 11th.

1959, his last full year as uncontested champion, was another rare low-profile year; in his two fights, he beat Sterling Davis by a knockout in three, and then Durelle again, also by a knockout in three, to once again retain his world light heavyweight title.

During 1960, Moore was stripped of his world light heavyweight title by the National Boxing Association (NBA), but continued to be recognized by most major boxing authorities including the New York State Athletic Commission and Ring Magazine. Moore won three of his four bouts in 1960, one by decision against Buddy Turman in Dallas, Texas, his lone loss coming in a ten-round decision versus Giulio Rinaldi in Rome.

In 1961, he defeated Turman again by decision in Manila, Philippines before defending his lineal world light heavyweight championship for what would be the last time, beating Rinaldi by a 15 round decision to retain the belt. In his last fight that year, he once again ventured into the heavyweights, and met Pete Rademacher, a man who had made history earlier in his career by becoming the first man ever to challenge for a world title in his first professional bout (when he lost to Patterson by a knockout in six). Moore beat Rademacher by a knockout in nine.

In 1962, the remaining boxing commissions that had continued to back Moore as the world light heavyweight champion withdrew their recognition. He campaigned exclusively as a heavyweight from then on, and beat Alejandro Lavorante by a knockout in 10 and Howard King by a knockout in one round in Tijuana. He then drew against future world light heavyweight champion Willie Pastrano in a 10-round heavyweight contest. Interestingly enough on the posters advertising that fight, Moore was billed as the "world light heavyweight champion." The bout took place in California which had not yet withdrawn recognition from Moore at the time the Moore-Pastrano fight was signed. By the time the bout took place, the California commission, like New York, Massachusetts, the EBU, and Ring Magazine, had recognized Harold Johnson, who had beaten Doug Jones 16 days earlier, as the new light heavyweight champ. Johnson had reigned as the NBA's (WBA's) champion since February 7, 1961.

Then, in his last fight of note, Moore faced a young heavyweight out of Louisville named Cassius Clay (Muhammad Ali). Moore had been Clay's trainer for a time, but Clay became dissatisfied and left Moore because of Moore's attempts to change his style, and his insistence that Clay do dishes and help clean gym floors.

In the days before the fight, Clay had rhymed that "Archie Moore...Must fall in four." Moore replied that he had perfected a new punch for the match: The Lip-Buttoner.

Nonetheless, as Clay predicted Moore was beaten by a knockout in four rounds. Moore is the only man to have faced both Rocky Marciano and Muhammad Ali.

After one more fight in 1963, a third round knockout win over Mike DiBiase in Phoenix, Moore announced his retirement from boxing, for good.

Final retirement

Despite retiring, Moore couldn't escape the limelight, and received numerous awards and dedications. In 1965, he was given the key to the city of San Diego, California.. In 1970, he was named "Man of The Year" by *Listen Magazine*, and received the key to the city of Sandpoint, Ohio.

He was elected in 1985 to the St. Louis city Boxing Hall of Fame, and he received the Rocky Marciano Memorial Award in the city of New York in 1988. In 1990, he became a member of the International Boxing Hall Of Fame in Canastota, being one of the original members of that institution.

The oldest boxer to win the world's light heavyweight crown, he is believed to have been the only boxer who boxed professionally in the eras of Joe Louis, Marciano and Muhammad Ali. He is one of only a handful of boxers whose careers spanned four decades; his final record was an astonishing 185 wins, 23 losses, 11 draws and 1 no contest, with 131 official knockouts.

However, at least three of Moore's record 131 knockouts came in less-than-competitive matches against pro wrestlers: "Professor" Roy Shire in 1956, Sterling Davis in 1959, and Mike DiBiase in 1963 (Moore's 131st and final knockout). All three matches are officially listed as third-round TKO stoppages. But even if one amends Moore's career numbers, he would still hold the record. The second-highest amount of knockouts in boxing history is 125, a total shared by light heavyweight Young Stribling and welterweight Billy Bird.

Acting career

In 1960, Moore was chosen to play the role of the runaway slave Jim in Michael Curtiz's film adaptation of Mark Twain's *The Adventures of Huckleberry Finn*, opposite Eddie Hodges as Huck. Moore garnered positive reviews for his sympathetic portrayal of Jim, which some viewers still consider the best interpretation of this much-filmed role.

Moore did not choose to pursue a full-time career as an actor, but he did appear in 1960s films such as *The Fortune Cookie* and *The Carpetbaggers* and on television in episodes of *Family Affair*, *Perry Mason*, *Wagon Train*, *The Reporter*, *Batman* and the soap opera *One Life to Live*. He made a brief return to film in 1975, playing a chef in *Breakheart Pass* with Charles Bronson, and had a cameo role as himself in the 1982 Jamaa Fanaka film *Penitentiary II*, along with Leon Isaac Kennedy and Mr. T.

Personal life

With his first wife Elizabeth A. Thorton, Moore had two children: Archie Moore Jr. and Betty Moore of City Heights, California.

Moore and second wife Joan Hardy Moore had five children - Reena Marie, Joanie Marie (J'Marie), Hardy Lee, D'Angello Greeg, and Anthony Cleveland - and raised an under-privileged youth as one of their own, Billy Ray McDaniel, one of many children Moore helped during his lifetime.

In 1997, J'Marie, became the first daughter of a famous boxer to herself become a professional boxer.

Death

Archie Moore died of heart failure in 1998 four days shy of his 85th birthday. He was cremated and is interred in a niche at Cypress View Mausoleum and Crematory, in San Diego.

Accolades

- In 1965, Moore was also inducted by the San Diego Hall of Champions into the Breitbard Hall of Fame [1].
- In 2002, Archie Moore was inducted into the St. Louis Walk of Fame.

- In 2006, Moore was inducted into the California Boxing Hall of Fame
- *Ring Magazine* ranked Moore #4 on its "Best Punchers of all time" list in 2003 and #14 on its list of the "80 Best Fighters of the Last 80 Years"

Further reading

- Mike Fitzgerald; Jake La Motta, Bert Randolph Sugar, Pete Ehrmann (2004). *The Ageless Warrior: The Life of Boxing Legend Archie Moore* [2] (illustrated ed.). Sports Publishing. ISBN 1582612552, 9781582612553.

External links

- Professional boxing record for Archie Moore [3] from BoxRec
- "Archie Moore" [4]. Find a Grave. Retrieved September 19, 2010.

Jimmy Bivins

Statistics	
Real name	James Louis Bivins
Rated at	Heavyweight
Nationality	American
Birth date	December 6, 1919
Birth place	Dry Branch, Georgia, U.S.
Stance	Orthodox
Boxing record	
Total fights	112
Wins	86
Wins by KO	31
Losses	25
Draws	1
No contests	0

James Louis Bivins, (born December 6, 1919) is a former American heavyweight boxer whose professional career ran from 1940 to 1955. He was born in Dry Branch, Gerogia. Although he was never given the opportunity to fight for a world title, despite at one point being the number one contender in both the light heavyweight and heavyweight divisions, Bivins fought and defeated many of the great fighters of his era. In recognition of his achievements in the ring - among other things, he defeated eight of the eleven world champions he faced - Bivins was inducted into the International Boxing Hall of Fame in 1999.

Boxing career

Although he was born in Georgia, Bivins fought out of Cleveland, Ohio for the entirety of his career. He made his professional debut on January 15, 1940, winning by knockout in the first round, and went on to win his first nineteen fights, all fought in 1940, before losing a split decision to Anton Christoforidis, whom he had previously beaten. Bivins won his first four fights of 1941, including contests with Teddy Yarosz and Curtis Sheppard, but lost three of his other four contests that year, which included a points loss to Melio Bettina. He began 1942 with wins against Billy Soose and Gus Lesnevich and a split-decision loss to Bob Pastor. After this loss, Bivins had a twenty-seven fight undefeated streak that lasted for four years; it was during this period that Bivins established himself as one of the great heavyweights of his era - a remarkable achievement given that, at 5' 9", he was often significantly smaller than his opponents.

Bivins first fight after losing to Pastor was a split-decision win against Joey Maxim, a fellow Cleveland fighter who went on to become a member of the hall of fame. Bivins fought four more contests in 1942, including a rematch with Bob Pastor and a bout with Lee Savold, and won them all. He began 1943 with a remarkable win against Ezzard Charles, in which he recorded seven knockdowns against the future heavyweight world champion. On February 23, 1943 he defeated Anton Christoforidis on points for the duration light heavyweight title - as all the world titles had been frozen for the duration of World War II, this was the closest he ever came to holding a world title. In the three years after this fight Bivins went on to defeat Tami Mauriello, Pat Valentino, Lloyd Marshall, Melio Bettina, Curtis Sheppard and Archie Moore, whom he knocked-down six times en route to a knockout victory. Bivins served with the United States Army from March, 1944 until his honorable discharge in November of the same year - during 1944 he fought only one professional fight, a points victory over Lee Q. Murray.

On February 25, 1946 Bivins fought Jersey Joe Walcott at the Cleveland Arena. The fight was Bivins' first loss in four years, the split decision was interesting in that one official had the fight 6-4 to Bivins, the second had it 9-1 to Walcott and the last had it 5-4-1 to Bivins but gave the fight to Walcott because of a third round knockdown in his favour. After losing his long unbeaten streak, Bivins' record as a fighter became somewhat average. After his loss to Walcott, Bivins went on to lose his next two contests, against Lee Q. Murray and Ezzard Charles, before winning the following four. Bivins suffered a knockout loss to Ezzard Charles on March 10, 1947 and went on to lose a further two of his final seven fights that year, to Lee Q. Murray and Archie Moore. He went on to win six of his nine fights in 1948, losing only to Joey Maxim, Ezzard Charles and Archie Moore. In 1949 he won five of his eight fights, but lost to both Archie Moore and Harold Johnson. He only fought twice in 1950, but returned to fighting regularly the following year. In 1951 he defeated Ted Lowry on points, but was once again knocked-out by Archie Moore and lost by unanimous decision to both Joe Louis and the undefeated Bob Baker. Bivins had a further eleven fights after his loss to Baker, and won eight of them. His only big-name opponent during these final fights was Ezzard Charles, who won by decision on November 26, 1952. Bivins retired following a victory over the journeyman Chubby Wright in June 1953, but returned for two final fights, both of which he won, a couple of years later.

References

- Professional boxing record for Jimmy Bivins [1] from BoxRec
- WCPN interview [2]
- thesweetscience.com biography [3]
- IBHOF citation [4]

Lloyd Marshall

Lloyd Marshall was a light heavyweight boxer who will be inducted posthumously into the International Boxing Hall of Fame in June 2010.

Pro career

Marshall began boxing at the age of 17 and turned pro in 1936. In 1943 Marshall fought for the "Duration" Light Heavyweight Title against Jimmy Bivins. During the bout, Bivins was knocked down in the 7th for a 2-count, and then Marshall was down for nine in the 9th, and at the bell in the 12th. Marhsall was then being counted out in the 13th to lose the bout. In 1944 he captured the Vacant "Duration" World Light Heavyweight Title with a victory over Nate Bolden. Due to the fact that he fought at his peak during World War II, Marshall never fought for an officially recognized world title. He retired in 1951 after KO losses to Bobo Olson and then Harry Matthews.

Honors

Marshall was inducted to World Boxing Hall of Fame in 1996. He is also set to be posthumously inducted to the International Boxing Hall of Fame in June 2010.

External links

- Professional boxing record for Lloyd Marshall [1] from BoxRec
- "Who I voted for in HOF election?" - ESPN.com [2]
- Cyber Boxing Zone page [3]

Famous Fights

Joe Baksi

Statistics	
Real name	Joseph William Baksi
Rated at	Heavyweight
Nationality	American
Birth date	January 14, 1922
Birth place	Kulpmont, Pennsylvania
Death date	August 6, 1977
Death place	Albany, New York
Stance	Orthodox
Boxing record	
Total fights	72
Wins	60
Wins by KO	29
Losses	9
Draws	3
No contests	0

Joe Baksi (January 14, 1922 – August 6, 1977) was a top heavyweight contender who defeated fighters such as Tami Mauriello, Lee Savold, Lou Nova, and Freddie Mills, while losing decisions to Jersey Joe Walcott and Ezzard Charles.

Background

Joe Baksi was a child of the Kulpmont, Pennsylvania coal mines. He was quoted as saying that he never had any intention of being a boxer, but he saw it "as a ticket to a better way of life, out of the coal mines." He broke into professional boxing in 1940 at the age of 18. He beat nine boxers that year, including the future movie actor Jack Palance (who fought under the name of *Jack Brazzo*) at the Westchester County Center in White Plains, NY.

Becoming a contender

Baksi campaigned over the boxing circuit for a number of years, until he got his first big match with Tami Mauriello on February 25, 1944 at Madison Square Garden. Mauriello was the 5-11 favorite, and the bronx contender for the Heavyweight crown. Mauriello was expected to win, based on his experience. Baski hoped to win by matching punch with punch and using his 210 vs. 196 lb weight advantage to his favor. Tami was floored late in the first round with a left hook by Baksi, and was down for a nine count. Tami faced a battering and battled back to prevent his first knockout defeat. Baksi won by unanimous decision.

Baksi's upset over Tami sprang him to nation-wide prominence. He was the favorite to beat Lee Savold two weeks later at the Garden, having the weight advantage and coming off his victory over Mauriello (who had beaten Savold twice before). But Baksi was a tyro compared to Savold. Baksi got off to a slow start, and though he showed advantage in the ninth and tenth rounds Savold boxed his way with left hooks and jabs to win a split decision that night. They had a rematch on March 10, 1944. This time, Savold was the 5-7 favorite. Baksi was in better shape that night, and fought a careful fight, out "left-handing" Savold, who was thought to have the best southpaw amongst the heavyweight contenders. At the finish Savold's left eye was cut, his nose and mouth bleeding, and his left side looked like raw hamburger. Baksi's only wound was a broken nose. He won a unanimous decision. His victory advanced him to be ranked 4th in the N.B.A rankings, behind champion Joe Louis, and boxers Billy Conn and Jimmy Bivins. Baksi went on to beat Savold again on August 7, 1944.

In his next fight, Baksi defeated Finnish boxer Gunnar (*GeeBee*) Baerlund and then scheduled a fight with his former sparring partner Lee Oma on January 28, 1945. Oma, unknown six months previously, gained fame by putting up a spirited fight against Mauriello in September. Oma lost that fight but earned a rematch in December, which he won. Still, Baksi was a 1-3 favorite to beat Oma. He had a 25-pound advantage over Oma, and corresponding advantages in height, reach, and punching power. But he lacked mental alertness that night, having suffered a cold over the last several days before the fight. He made a late comeback in the fight, but lost the fight by a unanimous decision.

Baksi went on to win a unanimous decision against Lou Nova on March 30, flooring Nova in the fourth round with a left hook to the ribs that kept Nova down for a count of nine. Baksi was now the second ranked (wartime) heavyweight. He scored easy decisions against Lee Dixie Oliver and Larry Lane, and then fought a thirty-one year old Jersey Joe Walcott. Walcott had lost earlier bouts with world-class professionals, and was an underdog against Baksi. But Walcott won, scoring 6-3-1 on the single referees scorecard. Walcott's dancing and dodging allowed him to escape Baksi's reach, and he was able to get in enough hooks to make Baksi groggy. Baksi lost his next fight with Jimmy Bell (a split decision in which Baksi was penalized two rounds for a low blow), but then racked up four easy wins before traveling to Europe.

🖳 **External images**	
🔍	Baksi in his prime [1]
🔍	Post Card [2]
🔍	Bow Tie Advert [3]

Europe and back

Baksi left for Europe on October 9, 1946 to fight the two British champions. He first defeated British light heavy weight champion Freddie Mills. Baksi was sluggish in the first round, but Mills (who had chronic eye problems) suffered a cut in his right eye in the second round, and his left eye in the third. After a bad battering, Mills gave up at the end of the sixth round. Baksi then went on to fight British heavyweight champion Bruce Woodcock. Baksi floored Woodcock three times in the first round and twice in the second. Woodcock made a comeback in the fifth, but Baksi was scoring at will when the referee stopped it in the seventh. Woodcock went to the hospital with a broken jaw.

After defeating Woodcock, Baksi was scheduled to fight Joe Louis for the world heavyweight title. Baksi, still in Europe after the Woodcock fight, signed a contract to fight the Swedish champion, Olle Tandberg in Stockholm. Baksi was the 1-5 favorite to beat Tandberg, and 1-3 favorite to knock him out by the seventh round. Baksi was going into the ring with 6 straight victories (five by knockout), while Tandberg had been fighting only since 1943, and only against local fighters. Then, in what the New York Times reported as the greatest upset in years, Baksi lost a split decision. Even Tandberg was surprised, saying after the fight "I didn't believe I had won the fight. I thought I was too much on the defensive in the closing rounds."

After his stunning defeat, Baksi took a year off. He was still the third ranked heavyweight contender, behind Jersey Joe Walcott and Ezzard Charles, and ahead of Lee Savold, when he scheduled a fight with Ezzard Charles. The winner of that fight would have a title match with Joe Louis. Charles, the 5-14 favorite, defeated Baksi by TKO in the seventh.

Later career

After being beaten by Charles, his status as a contender faded. After beating some obscure and aging boxers, he went into semi-retirement in 1951. He then made a comeback attempt in 1954, fighting Billy Smith, who he knocked out in the first round. His second match was with a tougher opponent, Bob "The Grinder" Baker, who was the 7-5 favorite. Baksi had little to offer except courage and stamina, and lost by unanimous decision. Baksi's manager, Leo Feureisen, collapsed during the fight and died in the dressing room a short while after. Baksi went into permanent retirement after the bout. He then became a teamster and later an ironworker and joined the International Brotherhood of Ironworkers.

Trivia

In the book *Trainspotting*, by Irvine Welsh, several of the characters use the phrase Joe Baksi to refer to a taxicab (taxi). The phrase is an example of rhyming slang and is used infrequently throughout the UK.

Sources

- Professional boxing record for Joe Baksi [4] from BoxRec
- MAURIELLO CHOICE TO VANQUISH BAKSI; Bronx Heavyweight Rated 5-7 Edge in Ten-Round Bout at the Garden Tonight [5]
- Baksi Outpoints Mauriello in 10-Round Upset Before 16,015 Fans at Garden; BRONX BOXER LOSES HEAVYWEIGHT BOUT Baksi Floors Mauriello for 9 in First and Carries On to Unanimous Decision BODY BLOWS WEAKEN TAMI Pennsylvanian Forces Action Throughout Spirited Fight [6]
- BAKSI 1-2 CHOICE TO DEFEAT SAVOLD; Hard-Hitting Heavyweights to Meet in Ten-Rounder at the Garden Tonight [7]
- Savold Beats Baksi in Heavyweight Bout Before 15,947 at Garden; DES MIOS BOXER GETS SPLIT VERDICT Savold Tags Onrushing Baksi With Left Hooks and Jabs to Win 10-Round Fight BOTH LAND HARD PUNCHES But No Knockdowns Result [8]
- SAVOLD 5-7 CHOICE TO VANQUISH BAKSI; Heavyweights to Meet Over 12-Round Route in Return Garden Bout Tonight [9]
- Baksi Decisively Outpoints Savold in 12-Round Heavyweight Bout at Garden; UNANIMOUS VERDICT FOR PENNSYLVANIAN Baksi's Sharp Left Helps Him Reverse Result of Previous Meeting With Savold [10]
- BAKSI PLACED 4TH IN N.B.A. RANKINGS; Conqueror of Savold Is Rated Behind Louis, Conn, Bivins [11]
- BAKSI BEATS SAVOLD ON POINTS IN CHICAGO [12]
- OMA BEATS BAKSI IN BOXING UPSET; THE WINNER FORCING THE FIGHTING [13]

- BAKSI BEATS NOVA WITH LATE RALLY; CALIFORNIA HEAVYWEIGHT ON THE FLOOR [14]
- WALCOTT OUTBOXES BAKSI; Notches Upset in Heavyweight Bout in Camden Ring [15]
- BAKSI STOPS MILLS AT END OF SIXTH; British Boxer Fails to Answer Bell for Seventh as Both Eyes Are Injured [16]
- AMERICAN BATTERS BRITISH CHAMPION; Baksi Drops Woodcock 5 Times in First 2 Rounds -- London Bout Stopped in Seventh VICTOR IN LINE FOR LOUIS Pennsylvanian Qualifies for World Title Fight [17]
- BAKSI TURNS DOWN MATCH WITH LOUIS; Walcott and Bettina Possible Rivals for Heavyweight Champion June 26 [18]
- BAKSI CHANGES HIS MIND; Now Says He Wants to Fight Louis in September [19]
- BAKSI 1-5 FAVORITE IN STOCKHOLM BOUT; U.S. Boxer to Meet Tandberg Today -- Winner to Get Match With Louis [20]
- DECISION AWARDED TO SWEDISH BOXER; Verdict for Tandberg Over Baksi Is Called 'Disgrace' by American's Manager SURPRISE TO THE VICTOR Didn't Think He Had Fought So Well -- Result Snarls Plans for Louis Title Bout [21]
- Charles Stops Baksi in Eleventh to Become Leading Contender for Louis' Title; 11,194 SEE REFEREE HALT GARDEN FIGHT Baksi, Blinded by Systematic Beating, Is Stopped in 2:33 of Eleventh by Charles [22]
- A Foe for Joe [23]
- BAKER SETS BACK BAKSI ON POINTS; Loser's Manager Dies After Ringside Collapse [24]
- Joe Baksi Dies at 55; Was a Top Heavyweight; Fought Charles, Walcott [25]

Jersey Joe Walcott

Statistics	
Real name	Arnold Raymond Cream
Nickname(s)	Jersey Joe
Rated at	Heavyweight
Height	6 ft 0 in (1.83 m)
Reach	74 in (188 cm)
Nationality	American
Birth date	January 31, 1914
Birth place	Merchantville, New Jersey, U.S.
Death date	February 25, 1994 (aged 80)
Death place	Camden, New Jersey, U.S.
Stance	Orthodox
Boxing record	
Total fights	71
Wins	51
Wins by KO	32
Losses	18
Draws	2
No contests	0

Arnold Raymond Cream (January 31, 1914 − February 25, 1994), better known as **Jersey Joe Walcott**, was a world heavyweight boxing champion. He broke the world's record for the oldest man to win the world's Heavyweight title when he earned it at the age of 37 years, 168 days.

Background

Walcott was born in Merchantville, New Jersey, the son of immigrants from Barbados. Walcott's father died when he was 13 years old, so he quit school and took a job working in a soup factory to support his mother and 11 siblings. He also began training as a boxer. He took the name of his boxing idol, Joe Walcott, the welterweight champion from Barbados, hence his nickname, "Jersey Joe".

Boxing career

He debuted as a professional boxer on September 9, 1930, fighting Cowboy Wallace and winning by a knockout in round one. After five straight knockout wins, in 1933, he lost for the first time, beaten on points by Henry Wilson in Philadelphia.

He built a record of 45 wins, 11 losses and 1 draw before challenging for the world title for the first time. Walcott lost early bouts against world-class competition. He lost a pair of fights to Tiger Jack Fox and was knocked out by contender Abe Simon. But that would change in 1945 when Walcott beat top heavyweights such as Joe Baksi, Lee Q. Murray, Curtis Sheppard and Jimmy Bivins. He closed out 1946 with a pair of losses to former light heavyweight champ Joey Maxim and heavyweight contender Elmer Ray, but promptly avenged those defeats in 1947.

On December 5, 1947, he fought Joe Louis, at thirty three years of age breaking the record as the oldest man to fight for the world heavyweight title. Despite dropping Louis in round one, and once again in round four, he lost a 15 round split decision. Most ringside observers and boxing writers felt Walcott deserved the win, and so there was a rematch on June 25, 1948, when Louis prevailed once again, this time by a knockout in round 11.

June 22 of 1949, Walcott got another chance to become world heavyweight champion, when he and Ezzard Charles met for the title left vacant by Louis. However, Charles prevailed, winning by decision in 15 rounds. Walcott, disappointed but eager to see his dream of being a champion come true, went on, and in 1950, he won four of his five bouts, including a three round knock-out of future world light heavyweight champion Harold Johnson.

On March 7 of 1951, he and Charles fought for a second time and once again Charles won a 15 round decision to retain his world title. But on July 18, he joined a handful of boxers who claimed the world title in their fifth try, when he knocked out Charles in seven rounds in Pittsburgh, to finally become world's heavyweight champion, at the relatively old age of 37. This made him the oldest man ever to win the world heavyweight crown (a distinction he would hold until George Foreman won the title at age 45 in 1994).

Walcott retained the title with a 15 round decision victory against arch-enemy Charles. On September 23, 1952, in spite of having a comfortable lead on his challenger, he lost his title to Rocky Marciano by knockout in round 13. There was a rematch in Chicago, on May 15, 1953, and the second time around, Walcott was again defeated by Marciano by a knockout in the first round.

Post boxing

He did not go away from the celebrity scene after boxing. In 1956, he co-starred with Humphrey Bogart and Max Baer in the boxing drama *The Harder They Fall*. In 1963, he tried professional wrestling, losing to Lou Thesz. Thesz pinned Walcott in the fifth round, but has stated that Walcott knocked him (Thesz) down and most likely out in that fifth round. As he fell to the floor, he relied on instinct, grabbing Walcotts knees, taking him down with him and stretching him out for the pin.

In 1965, he refereed the controversial world heavyweight championship bout between Muhammad Ali and Sonny Liston. Walcott lost the count as Ali circled around a floored Liston and Walcott tried to get him back to a neutral corner. Then Walcott looked outside the ring (presumably to the ringside count keeper) as Ali and Liston went at each other before Walcott instructed them to keep on fighting, then Walcott approached the fighters and abruptly stopped the fight. Walcott would never be appointed as a referee after this bout. It should be said, however, that most of the controversy surrounding this fight had nothing to do with Walcott, as this was the famous fight with the "phantom punch".

Walcott became Sheriff of Camden County in 1972 and then chairman of the New Jersey State Athletic Commission in 1975 until 1984, when he stepped down at the mandatory retirement age of 70. Walcott was inducted into the International Boxing Hall of Fame in Canastota.

See also

- List of heavyweight boxing champions
- List of WBA world champions

External Links

- Professional boxing record for Jersey Joe Walcott [1] from BoxRec
- Jersey Joe Walcott, Boxing Champion, Dies at 80 [2]
- Grave site [3]
- Left Hook Stops Charles in 7th, Makes Walcott Oldest Champ, The Milwaukee Journal, July 19, 1951 [4]
- Sport: Winner & New Champeen!, Time Magazine, July 30, 1951 [5]

Joe Louis

Statistics	
Real name	Joseph Louis Barrow
Nickname(s)	Brown Bomber
Rated at	Heavyweight
Height	6 ft 2 in (1.88 m)
Reach	76 in (190 cm)
Nationality	American
Birth date	May 13, 1914
Birth place	La Fayette, Alabama, USA
Death date	April 12, 1981 (aged 66)
Death place	Paradise, Nevada, USA
Stance	Orthodox
Boxing record	
Total fights	68
Wins	65
Wins by KO	51
Losses	3
Draws	0
No contests	1

Joseph Louis Barrow (May 13, 1914 − April 12, 1981), better known as **Joe Louis**, was the world heavyweight boxing champion from 1937 to 1949. Nicknamed the **Brown Bomber**, Louis helped elevate boxing from a nadir in popularity in the post-Jack Dempsey era by establishing a reputation as an honest, hardworking fighter at a time when the sport was dominated by gambling interests. Louis's championship reign lasted 140 consecutive months, during which he participated in 27 championship fights, including 25 successful title defenses – all records for the heavyweight division. In 2005, Louis was named the greatest heavyweight of all time by the International Boxing Research Organization, and was ranked number one on *The Ring*'s list of 100 Greatest Punchers of All Time.

Louis's cultural impact was felt well outside the ring. He is widely regarded as the first African American to achieve the status of a nationwide hero within the United States, and was also a focal point of anti-Nazi sentiment leading up to and during World War II. He also was instrumental in integrating the game of golf, breaking the sport's color barrier in America by appearing under a sponsor's exemption in a PGA event in 1952.

Early life

Louis was born on May 13, 1914 in a ramshackle dwelling about six miles northwest of La Fayette, in rural Chambers County, Alabama. Louis was the son of Munroe Barrow and Lillie (Reese) Barrow, and seventh of eight children. He weighed 11 pounds at birth. Both Louis's parents were the children of former slaves, alternating between sharecropping and rental farming. Munroe was predominantly African American with some white ancestry, while Lillie was half Cherokee.

Louis spent twelve years growing up in rural Alabama, where little is known of his childhood. He suffered from a speech impediment, and spoke very little until about the age of six. Munroe Barrow was committed to a mental institution in 1916, and as a result Joe knew very little of his biological father. Around 1920, Louis's mother married Pat Brooks, a local construction contractor, having received word that Munroe Barrow had died while institutionalized (in reality, Munroe Barrow lived until 1938, unaware of his son's fame).

In 1926, shaken by an altercation with the Ku Klux Klan, Louis's family moved to Detroit, Michigan, forming part of the post-World War I Great Migration. Joe's brother worked for Ford Motor Company (where Joe would himself work for a time at the River Rouge Plant) and the family settled into a home at 2700 Catherine (now Madison) Street in Detroit's Black Bottom neighborhood.

Louis attended Bronson Vocational School for a time to learn cabinet-making, and his mother attempted to get Joe interested in playing the violin.

Amateur career

The Depression hit the Louis family hard, but as an alternative to gang activity, Joe began to spend time at a local youth recreation center at 637 Brewster Street in Detroit. Legend has it that he tried to hide his pugilistic ambitions from his mother by carrying his boxing gloves inside his violin case.

Louis's amateur debut, probably in early 1932, came as a light-heavyweight at age 17. A legend exists that before the fight Louis, only barely literate, wrote his name so large that there was no room for his last name "Barrow" – as a result becoming known as "Joe Louis" for the remainder of his boxing career. More likely, Louis simply omitted his last name to keep his boxing pursuits a secret from his mother. After this debut (a loss to future Olympian Johnny Miller), Louis compiled numerous amateur victories – eventually winning the club championship of his Brewster Street recreation center, the home of many aspiring Golden Gloves fighters.

In 1933, Louis won the Detroit-area Golden Gloves Novice Division championship for the light heavyweight classification against Joe Biskey, later losing in the Chicago Golden Gloves Tournament of Champions. The next year, competing in the Golden Gloves' Open Division, he won the light heavyweight classification, this time also winning the Chicago Tournament of Champions. Although a hand injury forced Louis to miss the New York/Chicago Champions' cross-town bout for the ultimate Golden Gloves championship in 1934, he followed up his Chicago performance by winning the National AAU tournament in St. Louis, Missouri in April of that year. By the end of his amateur career, Louis's record was 50 wins against 4 losses, with 43 knockouts.

Professional career

Early years

Louis's impressive amateur performances attracted the interest of professional promoters. Rather than sign with an established promoter, Louis agreed to be represented by a black Detroit-area bookmaker named John Roxborough. As Louis explained it in his autobiography, Roxborough convinced Louis that white managers would have no real interest in seeing a black boxer work his way up to title contention:

> [Roxborough] told me about the fate of most black fighters, ones with white managers, who wound up burned-out and broke before they reached their prime. The white managers were not interested in the men they were handling but in the money they could make from them. They didn't take the proper time to see that their fighters had a proper training, that they lived comfortably, or ate well, or had some pocket change. Mr. Roxborough was talking about Black Power before it became popular.

Roxborough knew a Chicago-area boxing promoter named Julian Black, who already had a stable of mediocre boxers against which Louis could hone his craft – this time in the more lucrative heavyweight division. Once he was part of the management team, Black solicited Jack "Chappie" Blackburn, another Chicago native, as Louis's trainer. As a result, Louis' initial professional fights were all located in the Chicago area. His professional debut came on July 4, 1934 against Jack Kracken in the Bacon Casino on Chicago's south side. Louis earned $59 for knocking out Kracken in the first round. Louis won all 12 professional fights that year, 10 by way of knockout.

In September 1934, while promoting a Detroit-area "coming home" bout for Louis against Canadian Alex Borchuk, Roxborough was pressured by members of the Michigan State Boxing Commission to have Louis sign with white management. Roxborough refused, and continued advancing Louis's career with bouts against heavyweight contenders Art Sykes and Stanley Poreda.

When training for a fight against Lee Ramage, Louis noticed a young female secretary for the black newspaper *Chicago Defender* at the gym. After defeating Ramage, the secretary, Marva Trotter, was invited to the celebration party at Chicago's Grand Hotel. Trotter would later become Louis's first wife in 1935.

During this time, Louis also met a longtime associate who would eventually become his personal lawyer, Truman Gibson. As a young associate at a law firm hired by Julian Black, Gibson was charged with personally entertaining Louis during the pendency of business deals.

Title contention

Although Louis' management was finding him bouts against legitimate heavyweight contenders, no path to the title was forthcoming. Although boxing was not officially segregated, white Americans had become wary of the prospect of another black champion in the wake of Jack Johnson's highly unpopular "reign of terror" atop the heavyweight division, and an informal barrier existed that kept black boxers out of title contention. Biographer Gerald Astor stated that "Joe Louis' early boxing career was stalked by the spectre of Jack Johnson."

A change in management was inevitable. In 1935, boxing promoter Mike Jacobs sought out Louis' handlers. After Louis' narrow defeat of Natie Brown on March 29, 1935, Jacobs and the Louis team met at the Frog Club, a colored nightclub, and negotiated a three-year exclusive boxing promotion deal. The contract, however, did not keep Roxborough and Black from attempting to cash in as Louis' managers; when Louis turned 21 on May 13, 1935, Roxborough and Black each signed Louis to an onerous long-term contract that collectively dedicated half of Louis' future income to the pair.

Black and Roxborough did, however, shape Louis' media image carefully and deliberately. Seeking to ensure that Louis did not meet the same fate as Johnson, who suffered tremendous public backlash for his flamboyant lifestyle, they drafted seven "commandments" for Louis' personal conduct. These included:

• Never have his picture taken with a white woman (though he once was photographed with a white teenaged girl for a local paper in Michigan who was doing a story on Louis for her high school newspaper).

- Never gloat over a fallen opponent
- Never engage in fixed fights
- Live and fight clean

As a result, Louis was generally portrayed in the white media as a clean-living, modest person, which facilitated his burgeoning celebrity status.

With the backing of major promotion, Louis fought 13 times in 1935. The bout that helped put him in the media spotlight occurred on June 25, when Louis knocked out a former world heavyweight champion, the 6'6", 265-pound Primo Carnera, in six rounds. Foreshadowing the Louis-Schmeling rivalry to come, the Carnera bout featured a political dimension. Louis' defeat of Carnera, who symbolized Benito Mussolini's regime in the popular eye, was seen as a victory for the international community, particularly among African Americans, who were sympathetic to Ethiopia during its occupation by Italy. America's white press began promoting Louis' image in as positive a manner as was possible for the times; nicknames created for Louis included the "mahogany mauler," "chocolate chopper," "coffee-colored KO king," "saffra sandman," and one that stuck, "The Brown Bomber."

Helping the white press to overcome any reluctance to feature a black contender was the fact that boxing, in the mid-1930s, was in desperate need of a marketable hero. Since the retirement of Jack Dempsey in 1929, boxing had devolved into a sordid mixture of poor athletes, gambling, fixed fights, thrown matches, and control of the sport by organized crime. *New York Times* columnist Edward VanNess wrote, "Louis ... is a boon to boxing. Just as Dempsey led the sport out of the doldrums ... so is Louis leading the boxing game out of a slump." Likewise, biographer Bill Libby asserted that "The sports world was hungry for a great champion when Louis arrived in New York in 1935."

Although the mainstream press was beginning to embrace Louis, there remained some fear at the prospect of another black heavyweight champion. In September 1935, on the eve of Louis' fight with the former title holder Max Baer, *Washington Post* sportswriter Shirley Povich expressed American hopes for the white contender; "They say Baer will surpass himself in the knowledge that he is the lone white hope for the defense of Nordic superiority in the prize ring." It was not to be. Although Baer had been knocked down only once before in his professional career (by Frankie Campbell), Louis dominated Baer, knocking him out in four rounds. Unknowingly, Baer suffered from a unique disadvantage in the fight; earlier that evening, Louis had married Marva Trotter at a friend's apartment, and was eager to end the fight in order to consummate the relationship. Later that year, Louis also knocked out Paolino Uzcudun, who had never been knocked down or out before.

Louis vs. Schmeling I

Main article: Joe Louis vs. Max Schmeling

By this time, Louis was ranked as the No. 1 contender in the heavyweight division, and had won the Associated Press' "Athlete of the Year" award for 1935. What was considered to be a final tune-up bout before an eventual title shot was scheduled for June 1936 against former world heavyweight champion Max Schmeling. Although a former champion, Schmeling was not considered a threat to Louis, then with an undefeated professional record of 27-0. Schmeling had won

Louis vs. Schmeling, 1936

his title on a technicality when Jack Sharkey was disqualified after giving Schmeling a low blow in 1930. Schmeling was also 30 years old at the time of the Louis bout, and allegedly past his prime. Perhaps as a result, Louis took his training for the Schmeling fight less than seriously. Louis's training retreat was located at Lakewood, New Jersey, where Louis was first able to practice the game of golf, which later became a lifelong passion. Noted entertainer Ed Sullivan had initially sparked Louis's interest in the sport by giving an instructional book to Joe's wife, Marva. Louis spent significant time on the golf course rather than training for the Schmeling match.

Conversely, Schmeling prepared intently for the bout. Schmeling had thoroughly studied Louis's style, and believed he had found a weakness. By exploiting Louis's habit of dropping his left hand low after a jab, Schmeling handed Louis his first professional loss by knocking him out in Round 12 at Yankee Stadium on June 19, 1936.

World Championship

After defeating Louis, Schmeling expected a title shot against James J. Braddock, who had unexpectedly defeated Max Baer for the heavyweight title the previous June. Madison Square Garden (MSG) had a contract with Braddock for the title defense and also sought a Braddock-Schmeling title bout. But Jacobs and Braddock's manager Joe Gould had been planning a Braddock-Louis matchup for months. Schmeling's victory gave Gould tremendous leverage, however; if he were to offer Schmeling the title chance instead of Louis, there was a very real possibility that Nazi authorities would never allow Louis a shot at the title. Gould's demands were therefore onerous: Jacobs would have to pay 10% of all future boxing promotion profits (including any future profits from Louis's future bouts) for ten years. Braddock and Gould would eventually receive more than $150,000 from this arrangement. Well before the actual fight, Jacobs and Gould publicly announced that their fighters would face for the heavyweight title on June 22, 1937. Figuring that the New York State Athletic Commission would not sanction the fight in deference to MSG and Schmeling, Jacobs scheduled the fight for Chicago.

Each of the parties involved worked to facilitate the controversial Braddock-Louis matchup. Louis did his part by knocking out former champion Jack Sharkey on August 18, 1936. Meanwhile, Gould trumped up anti-Nazi sentiment against Schmeling, and Jacobs defended a lawsuit by MSG to halt the Braddock-Louis fight. A federal court in Newark, New Jersey eventually ruled that Braddock's contractual obligation to stage his title defense at MSG was unenforceable for lack of mutual consideration.

The stage was set for Louis's title shot. On the night of the fight, June 22, 1937, Braddock was able to knock Louis down in Round 1, but afterward could accomplish little. After inflicting constant punishment, Louis defeated the "Cinderella Man" by knockout in Round 8. Louis's ascent to the world heavyweight title was complete.

Louis's victory was a seminal moment in African American history. Thousands of African Americans stayed up all night across the country in celebration. Noted author and member of the Harlem Renaissance Langston Hughes described Louis's effect in these terms:

> Each time Joe Louis won a fight in those depression years, even before he became champion, thousands of colored Americans on relief or W.P.A., and poor, would throng out into the streets all across the land to march and cheer and yell and cry because of Joe's one-man triumphs. No one else in the United States has ever had such an effect on Negro emotions – or on mine. I marched and cheered and yelled and cried, too.

Initial title defenses

Despite now being heavyweight champion, Louis was haunted by the earlier defeat to Schmeling. Shortly after winning the title, he was quoted as saying, "I don't want to be called champ until I whip Max Schmeling." Louis's manager Mike Jacobs attempted to arrange a rematch with Schmeling in 1937, but negotiations broke down when Schmeling demanded 30% of the gate. When Schmeling instead attempted to arrange for a fight against British Empire Champion Tommy Farr, known as the "Tonypandy Terror,"—ostensibly for a world championship to rival the claims of American boxing authorities—Jacobs outmaneuvered him, offering Farr a guaranteed $60,000 to fight Louis instead. The offer was too lucrative for Farr to turn down.

On August 30, 1937, after a postponement of four days due to rain, Louis and Farr finally touched gloves at New York's Yankee Stadium before a crowd of approximately 32,000. Louis fought one of the hardest battles of his life. The bout was closely contested and went the entire 15 rounds, with Louis being unable to knock Farr down. Referee Arthur Donovan was even seen shaking Farr's hand after the bout, in apparent congratulation. Nevertheless, after the score was announced, Louis had won a controversial unanimous decision. *Time* described the scene thus: "After collecting the judges' votes, referee Arthur Donovan announced that Louis had won the fight on points. The crowd of 50,000...amazed that Farr had not been knocked out or even knocked down, booed the decision... Speaking over the radio after the fight, Louis admitted that he had been hurt twice."

In preparation for the inevitable rematch with Schmeling, Louis tuned up with bouts against Nathan Mann and Harry Thomas.

Louis vs. Schmeling II

The rematch between Louis and Schmeling is one of the most famous boxing matches of all time, and is remembered as one of the major sports events of the 20th century. Following his defeat of Louis in 1936, Schmeling became a national hero in Germany. Schmeling's victory over an African American was touted by Nazi officials as proof of their doctrine of Aryan superiority. When the rematch was scheduled, Louis retreated to his boxing camp in New Jersey and trained incessantly for the fight. A few weeks before the bout, Louis visited the White House, where President Franklin D. Roosevelt told him, "Joe, we need muscles like yours to beat Germany." Louis later admitted: "I knew I had to get Schmeling good. I had my own personal reasons and the whole damned country was depending on me."

When Schmeling arrived in New York in June, 1938 for the rematch, he was accompanied by a Nazi party publicist who issued statements that a black man could not defeat Schmeling, and that when Schmeling won, his prize money would be used to build tanks in Germany. Schmeling's hotel was picketed by anti-Nazi protesters in the days before the fight.

On the night of June 22, 1938, Louis and Schmeling met for the second time in the boxing ring. The fight was held in Yankee Stadium before a crowd of 70,043. It was broadcast by radio to millions of listeners throughout the world, with radio announcers reporting on the fight in English, German, Spanish, and Portuguese. Before the bout, Schmeling weighed in at 193 pounds; Louis weighed in at 198¾ pounds.

The fight lasted two minutes and four seconds. Louis battered Schmeling with a series of swift attacks, forcing Schmeling against the ropes and giving him a paralyzing body blow (Schmeling later claimed it was an illegal kidney punch). Schmeling was knocked down three times, and only managed to throw two punches in the entire bout. On the third knockdown, Schmeling's trainer threw in the towel and referee Arthur Donovan stopped the fight.

"Bum of the Month Club"

In the 29 months from January 1939 through May 1941, Louis defended his title thirteen times, a frequency unmatched by any heavyweight champion since the end of the bare-knuckle era. The pace of his title defenses, combined with his convincing wins, earned Louis' opponents from this era the collective nickname "Bum of the Month Club". Notables of this lambasted pantheon include:

- World light-heavyweight champion John Henry Lewis who, attempting to move up a weight class, was knocked out in the first round by Louis on January 25, 1939.
- "Two Ton" Tony Galento, who was able to push Louis to the canvas in the third round of their bout on June 28, 1939, before letting his guard down and being knocked out in the fourth.

- Chilean Arturo Godoy, who Louis fought twice in 1940, on February 9 and June 20. Louis won the first bout by a decision, and the rematch by a knockout in the eighth round.
- Al McCoy, putative New England heavyweight champion, whose fight against Louis is probably best known for being the first heavyweight title bout held in Boston, Massachusetts (at the Boston Garden on December 16, 1940). The popular local challenger dodged his way around Louis before being unable to respond to the sixth-round bell.
- Clarence "Red" Burman, who pressed Louis for nearly five rounds at Madison Square Garden on January 31, 1941 before succumbing to a series of body blows.
- Gus Dorazio, of whom Louis remarked, "At least he tried," after being leveled by a short right hand in the second round at Philadelphia's Convention Hall on February 17.
- Abe Simon, who endured thirteen rounds of punishment before 18,908 at Olympia Stadium in Detroit on March 21 before referee Sam Hennessy declared a TKO.
- Tony Musto, who, at 5'7½" and 198 pounds, was known as the "baby tank". Despite a unique crouching style, Musto was slowly worn down over eight and a half rounds in St. Louis on April 8.
- Buddy Baer (brother of former champion Max), who was leading the May 23, 1941, bout in Washington, D.C., until an eventual barrage by Louis, capped by a late hit after the sixth round bell. Despite the late hit, referee Arthur Donovan disqualified Baer before the beginning of the seventh round as a result of stalling by Baer's manager.

Despite its derogatory nickname, most of the group were top-ten heavyweights. Of the twelve fighters Louis faced during this period, five were rated by *The Ring* as top-ten heavyweights in the year they fought Louis: Galento (overall #2 heavyweight in 1939), Bob Pastor (#3, 1939), Godoy (#3, 1940), Simon (#6, 1941), and Baer (#8, 1941); four others (Musto, Dorazio, Burman, and Johnny Paycheck) were ranked in the top ten in a different year.

Billy Conn fight

Louis' string of lightly-regarded competition ended with his bout against Billy Conn, the light-heavyweight champion and a highly-regarded contender. The fighters met on June 18, 1941, in front of a crowd of 54,487 fans at the Polo Grounds in New York City. The fight turned out to be one of the greatest heavyweight boxing fights of all time.

Conn would not gain weight for the challenge against Louis, saying instead that he would rely on a "hit and run" strategy. Louis's famous response: "He can run, but he can't hide."

However, Louis had clearly underestimated Conn's threat. In his autobiography, Joe Louis said, "I made a mistake going into that fight. I knew Conn was kinda small and I didn't want them to say in the papers that I beat up on some little guy so the day before the fight I did a little roadwork to break a sweat and drank as little water as possible so I could weigh in under 200 pounds. Chappie was as mad as hell. But Conn was a clever fighter, he was like a mosquito, he'd sting and move."

Conn had the better of the fight through twelve rounds, although Louis was able to stun Conn with a left hook in the fifth, cutting his eye and nose. By the eighth round, Louis began suffering from dehydration. By the twelfth round, Louis was exhausted, with Conn ahead on two of three boxing scorecards. But against the advice of his corner, Conn continued to closely engage Louis in the later stages of the fight. Louis made the most of the opportunity, knocking Conn out with two seconds left in the thirteenth round.

The contest created an instant rivalry that Louis's career had lacked since the Schmeling era, and a rematch with Conn was planned for late 1942. The rematch had to be abruptly canceled, however, after Conn broke his hand in a much-publicized fight with his father-in-law, major league ballplayer "Greenfield" Jimmy Smith. By the time Conn was ready for the rematch, the Japanese attack on Pearl Harbor had taken place, detouring Louis's heavyweight career.

World War II

Louis fought a charity bout for the Navy Relief Society against his former opponent Buddy Baer on January 9, 1942, which generated $47,000 for the fund. The next day, he volunteered to enlist as a private in the United States Army at Camp Upton, Long Island. Newsreel cameras recorded his induction, including a staged scene in which a soldier-clerk asked, "What's your occupation?" and Louis replied in a nervous rush, "Fighting and let us at them Japs."

Another military charity bout on March 27, 1942, (against another former opponent, Abe Simon) netted $36,146. Before the fight, Louis had spoken at a Relief Fund dinner, saying of the war effort: "We'll win, 'cause we're on God's side." The media widely reported the comment, instigating a surge of popularity for Louis. Slowly, the press would begin to eliminate its stereotypical racial references when covering Louis, and instead treat him as an unqualified sports hero. Despite the public relations boon, Louis's charitable fights would prove financially costly. Although Louis saw none of the roughly $90,000 raised by these and other charitable fights, the IRS would later credit these amounts as taxable income paid to Louis. After the war, the IRS would pursue the issue.

For basic training, Louis was assigned to a segregated cavalry unit based in Fort Riley, Kansas. The assignment was at the suggestion of his friend and lawyer Truman Gibson, who knew of Louis's love for horsemanship. Gibson had previously become a civilian advisor to the War Department, in charge of investigating claims of harassment against black soldiers. Accordingly, Louis used this personal connection to help the cause of various black soldiers with whom he came in to contact. In one noted episode, Louis contacted Gibson in order to facilitate the Officer Candidate School (OCS) applications of a group of African Americans at Fort Riley, which had been inexplicably delayed for several months. Among the OCS applications Louis facilitated turned out to be that of a young Jackie Robinson, later to break the baseball color barrier. The episode would spawn a personal friendship between the two men.

Realizing Louis's potential for elevating *esprit de corps* among the troops, the Army placed him in its Special Services Division rather than deploying him into combat. Louis would go on a celebrity tour with other notables including fellow boxer Sugar Ray Robinson. Louis traveled more than 21,000 miles and staged 96 boxing exhibitions before two million soldiers. In England during 1944, he was reported to have enlisted as a player for Liverpool Football Club as a publicity stunt.

In addition to his travels, Louis was the focus of a media recruitment campaign encouraging African-American men to enlist in the Armed Services, despite the military's racial segregation. When asked about his decision to enter the racially-segregated U.S. Army, Louis' explanation was simple: "Lots of things wrong with America, but Hitler ain't going to fix them." In 1943, Louis made an appearance in the wartime Hollywood musical *This Is the Army*, directed by Michael Curtiz. Louis appears as himself in a musical number, "The Well-Dressed Man In Harlem," which emphasizes the importance of African-American soldiers and promotes their enlistment.

Louis's celebrity power was not, however, merely directed toward African Americans. In a famous wartime recruitment slogan, Louis echoed his prior comments of 1942: "We'll win, because we're on God's side." The publicity of the campaign made Louis widely popular stateside, even outside the world of sports. Never before had white Americans embraced a black man as their representative to the world.

Although Louis never saw combat, his military service would see challenges of its own. During his travels he would often experience blatant racism. On one occasion, a military policeman (MP) ordered Louis and Ray Robinson to move their seats to a bench in the rear of an Alabama Army camp bus depot. "We ain't moving," said Louis. The MP tried to arrest them, but Louis forcefully argued the pair out of the situation. In another incident, Louis allegedly had to resort to bribery to persuade a commanding officer to drop charges against Jackie Robinson for punching a captain who had called Robinson a "nigger".

Louis was eventually promoted to the rank of sergeant, and was awarded the Legion of Merit medal for "incalculable contribution to the general morale." Receipt of the honor qualified Louis for immediate release from military service on October 1, 1945.

Later career and retirement

Louis emerged from his wartime service significantly in debt. In addition to his looming tax bill — which had not been finally determined at the time, but was estimated at greater than $100,000 — Jacobs claimed that Louis owed him $250,000.

Despite the financial pressure on Louis to resume boxing, his long-awaited rematch against Billy Conn had to be postponed to the summer of 1946, when weather conditions could accommodate a large outdoor audience. On June 19, a disappointing 40,000 saw the rematch at Yankee Stadium, in which Louis was not seriously tested. Conn, whose skills had deteriorated during the long layoff, largely avoided contact until being dispatched by knockout in the eighth round. Although the attendance did not meet expectations, the fight was still the most profitable of Louis's career to date. His share of the purse was $600,000, of which Louis' managers got $140,000, his ex-wife $66,000, and the state of New York $30,000.

After trouble finding another suitable opponent, on December 5, 1947, Louis met Jersey Joe Walcott, a 33-year-old veteran with a 44-11-2 record. Walcott entered the fight as a 10-to-1 underdog. Nevertheless, Walcott downed Louis twice in the first four rounds. Most observers in Madison Square Garden felt Walcott dominated the 15-round fight; when Louis was declared the winner in a split decision, the crowd booed.

Louis was under no delusion about the state of his boxing skills, yet he was too embarrassed to quit after the Walcott fight. Determined to win and retire with his title intact, Louis signed on for a rematch. On June 25, 1948, about 42,000 people came to Yankee Stadium to see the aging champion, who weighed 213½, the heaviest of his career to date. Walcott downed Louis in the third round, but Louis survived to knock Walcott out in the eleventh.

Louis would not defend his title again before announcing his retirement from boxing on March 1, 1949. In his bouts with Conn and Walcott, it had become apparent that Louis was no longer the fighter he once had been. As he had done earlier in his career, however, Louis would continue to appear in numerous exhibition matches worldwide.

Post-retirement comeback

At the time of Louis's initial retirement, the IRS was still completing its investigation of his prior tax returns, which had always been handled by Mike Jacobs's personal accountant. In May 1950, the IRS finished a full audit of Louis's past returns and announced that, with interest and penalties, he owed the government more than $500,000. Louis had no choice but to return to the ring.

After asking Gibson to take over his personal finances and switching his management from Jacobs and Roxborough to Marshall Miles, the Louis camp negotiated a deal with the IRS under which Louis would come out of retirement, with all Louis's net proceeds going to the IRS. A match with Ezzard Charles — who had acquired the vacant heavyweight title in June 1949 by outpointing Walcott — was set for September 27, 1950. By then, Louis was 36 years old, and had been away from competitive boxing for two years. Weighing in at 218, Louis was still strong, but his reflexes were gone. Charles repeatedly beat him to the punch. By the end of the fight, Louis was cut above both eyes, one of which was shut tight by swelling. He knew he had lost even before Charles was declared the winner. The result was not the only disappointing aspect of the fight for Louis; only 22,357 spectators paid to witness the event at Yankee Stadium, and his share of the purse was a mere $100,458. Louis had to continue fighting.

After facing several club-level opponents, the International Boxing Club guaranteed Louis $300,000 to face undefeated heavyweight contender Rocky Marciano on October 26, 1951. Despite his being a 6-to-5 favorite, few boxing insiders believed Louis had a chance. Marciano himself was reluctant to participate in the bout, but was understanding of Louis's position: "This is the last guy on earth I want to fight." It was feared, particularly among those who had witnessed Marciano's punching power first hand, that Louis's unwillingness to quit would result in serious injury. Fighting back tears, Ferdie Pacheco said in the *SportsCentury* documentary about his bout with Marciano, "He [Louis] wasn't just going to lose. He was going to take a vicious, savage beating. Before the eyes of the nation, Joe Louis, an American hero if ever there was one, was going to get beaten up." Louis was dropped in the eighth round by a Marciano left, and knocked out of the ring less than thirty seconds later.

In the dressing room after the fight, Louis's Army touring companion, Sugar Ray Robinson, wept. Marciano also attempted to console Louis, saying, "I'm sorry, Joe." "What's the use of crying?" Louis said. "The better man won. I guess everything happens for the best."

After facing Marciano, with the prospect of another significant payday all but gone, Louis retired for good from professional boxing. He would, as before, continue to tour on the exhibition circuit, with his last contest taking place on December 16, 1951, in Taipei, Taiwan, against Corporal Buford J. deCordova.

Taxes and financial troubles

Despite Louis's lucrative purses over the years, most of the proceeds went to his handlers. Of the over $4.6 million earned during his boxing career, Louis himself received only about $800,000. Louis was nevertheless extremely generous to his family, paying for homes, cars and education for his parents and siblings, often with money fronted by Jacobs. He invested in a number of businesses, all of which eventually failed, including the Joe Louis Restaurant, the Joe Louis Insurance Company, a softball team called the Brown Bombers, Joe Louis Milk Company, Joe Louis Punch (a drink), the Louis-Rower P.R. firm, a horse farm, and the Rhumboogie Café in Chicago. He gave liberally to the government as well, paying back the city of Detroit for any welfare money his family had received.

A combination of this largesse and government intervention eventually put Louis in severe financial straits. His entrusting of his finances to former manager Mike Jacobs haunted him. After the $500,000 IRS tax bill was assessed, with interest accumulating every year, the need for cash precipitated Louis's post-retirement comeback. Even though his comeback earned him significant purses, the incremental tax rate in place at the time (90%) meant that these boxing proceeds did not even keep pace with interest on Louis's tax debt. As a result, by the end of the 1950s, he owed over $1 million in taxes and interest. In 1953, when Louis's mother died, the IRS appropriated the $667 she had willed to Louis. To bring in money, Louis engaged in numerous activities outside the ring. He appeared on various quiz shows, and an old Army buddy, Ash Resnick, gave Louis a job welcoming tourists to the Caesars Palace hotel in Las Vegas, where Resnick was an executive. For income, Louis even became a professional wrestler in the 1950s and 60s, and again as late as 1972.

Louis remained a popular celebrity in his twilight years. His friends included former rival Max Schmeling—who provided Louis with financial assistance during his retirement—and mobster Frank

Lucas, who, disgusted with the government's treatment of Louis, once paid off a $50,000 tax lien held against him. These payments, along with an eventual agreement in the early 1960s by the IRS to limit its collections to an amount based on Louis's current income, allowed Louis to live comfortably toward the end of his life.

Professional golf

One of Louis's other passions was the game of golf, in which he also played a historic role. He was a long-time devotee of the sport since being introduced to the game before the first Schmeling fight in 1936. Similar to subsequent black athletes such as Michael Jordan and Charles Barkley, Louis was also known to mix gambling with his golf game. In 1952, Louis was invited to play in the San Diego Open on a sponsor's exemption, becoming the first African American to play a PGA Tour event. Initially, the PGA of America was reluctant to allow Louis to enter the event, having a bylaw at the time limiting PGA participation to Caucasians. However, Louis's celebrity eventually pushed the PGA toward removing the bylaw, paving the way for the first generation of African-American professional golfers such as Calvin Peete. Louis himself financially supported the careers of several other early black professional golfers, such as Bill Spiller, Ted Rhodes, Howard Wheeler, Clyde Martin and Charlie Sifford. He was also instrumental in founding The First Tee, a charity helping underprivileged children become acquainted with the game of golf. His son, Joe Louis Barrow, Jr., currently oversees the organization.

In 2009, the PGA of America granted posthumous membership to Ted Rhodes, John Shippen, and Bill Spiller, who were denied the opportunity to become PGA members during their professional careers. The PGA also has granted posthumous honorary membership to Louis.

Personal life and death

Louis had two children by wife Marva Trotter (daughter Jacqueline in 1943 and son Joseph Louis Barrow, Jr. in 1947) and adopted three others. They divorced in March 1945 only to remarry a year later, but were again divorced in February 1949. Marva moved on to an acting and modeling career. On Christmas Day 1955, Louis married Rose Morgan, a successful Harlem businesswoman; their marriage was annulled in 1958. Louis's final marriage − to Martha Jefferson, a lawyer from Los Angeles, on St. Patrick's Day 1959 − lasted until his death. They had a child and also named him Joe, Jr. The younger Joe Louis Barrow, Jr. lives in New York city and is involved in boxing.

Though married four times, Louis discreetly enjoyed the company of both African-American and white women, including Lena Horne, Sonja Henie, and Lana Turner.

Joe Louis' headstone in
Arlington National Cemetery,
Virginia

In 1953, Robert Gordon directed a movie about Louis's life, *The Joe Louis Story.* The movie, filmed in Hollywood, starred Golden Gloves fighter Coley Wallace in the role of Louis.

Starting in the 1960s, Louis was frequently mocked by segments of the African-American community (including Muhammad Ali) for being an Uncle Tom.

Drugs took a toll on Louis in his later years. In 1969, he was hospitalized after collapsing on a New York City street. While the incident was at first credited to "physical breakdown," underlying problems would soon surface. In 1970, he spent five months at the Colorado Psychiatric Hospital and the Veterans Administration Hospital in Denver, hospitalized by his wife, Martha, and his son, Joe Louis Barrow Jr., for paranoia. In a 1971 book, *Brown Bomber,* by Barney Nagler, Louis disclosed the truth about these incidents, stating that his collapse in 1969 had been caused by cocaine, and that his subsequent hospitalization had been prompted by his fear of a plot to destroy him. Strokes and heart ailments caused Louis's condition to deteriorate further later in the decade. He had surgery to correct an aortic aneurysm in 1977 and thereafter used an Amigo POV/scooter for a mobility aid.

Louis died of a heart attack in Desert Springs Hospital on April 12, 1981, just hours after his last public appearance viewing the Larry Holmes-Trevor Berbick heavyweight championship. Ronald Reagan waived the eligibility rules for burial at Arlington National Cemetery, and Louis was buried there with full military honors on April 21, 1981. His funeral was paid for in part by former competitor and friend, Max Schmeling, who also acted as a pallbearer.

Legacy

In all, Louis made 25 defenses of his heavyweight title from 1937 to 1948, and was a world champion for 11 years and 10 months. Both are still records in the heavyweight division, the former in any division. His most remarkable record is that he knocked out 23 opponents in 27 title fights, including 5 world champions. In addition to his accomplishments inside the ring, Louis uttered two of boxing's most famous observations: "He can run, but he can't hide" and "Everyone has a plan until they've been hit."

Louis is also remembered in sports outside of boxing. An indoor sports venue is named after him in Detroit, the Joe Louis Arena, where the Detroit Red Wings play their NHL games. In 1936, a beat writer for the *Winnipeg Tribune* used Joe Louis's nickname to refer to the Winnipeg Football Club after a game. From that point, the team became known popularly as the Winnipeg Blue Bombers.

Congressional Gold Medal in 1982

His recognition also transcends the sporting world. In 2002, scholar Molefi Kete Asante listed Joe Louis on his list of 100 Greatest African Americans. On August 26, 1982, Louis was posthumously approved for the Congressional Gold Medal, the highest award given to civilians by the U.S. legislative branch. Congress stated that he "did so much to bolster the spirit of the American people during one of the most crucial times in American history and which have endured throughout the years as a symbol of strength for the nation." Following Louis' death, President Ronald Reagan said, "Joe Louis was more than a sports legend -- his career was an indictment of racial bigotry and a source of pride and inspiration to millions of white and black people around the world."

A memorial to Louis was dedicated in Detroit (at Jefferson Avenue & Woodward) on October 16, 1986. The sculpture, commissioned by Time, Inc. and executed by Robert Graham, is a 24-foot-long (7.3 m) arm with a fisted hand suspended by a 24-foot-high (7.3 m) pyramidal framework. It represents the power of his punch both inside and outside the ring. Because of his efforts to fight Jim Crow laws, the fist was symbolically aimed toward the south.

On February 27, 2010, an 8-foot (2.4 m) bronze statue of Louis was unveiled in his Alabama hometown. The statue sits on a base of red granite outside the Chambers County Courthouse.

In 1993, he became the first boxer to be honored on a postage stamp issued by the U.S. Postal Service.

Various other facilities have been named after Joe Louis. A street near Madison Square Garden is named in his honor. The former Pipe O' Peace Golf Course in Riverdale, Illinois, (a Chicago suburb) was in 1986 renamed "Joe Louis The Champ Golf Course". American Legion Post 375 in Detroit is also named after Joe Louis.

In one of the most widely-quoted tributes to Louis, *New York Post* sportswriter Jimmy Cannon was known for the following statement (interjecting to another person's characterization of Louis as "a credit to his race"); "Yes, Joe Louis is a credit to his race—the human race."

In 2009, the band Yeasayer came out with a song titled "Ambling Alp" which imagines what advice Joe Louis's father might have given him prior to becoming a prizefighter. The song references adversities and opponents, including Max Schmeling and Primo Carnera, Louis had to overcome in his career.

Professional record

65 Wins (51 knockouts, 13 decisions, 1 disqualification), **3 Losses** (2 knockouts, 1 decision) Source: BoxRec.com [1]**Res.**Loss Win Win Win Win Win Win Win Win Loss Win Win Win Win Win Win Win Win Win Win Win Win Win Win Win Win Win Win Win Win Win Win Win Win Win Win Win Win Win Win Win Win Loss Win Win Win Win Win Win Win Win Win Win Win Win Win Win Win Win Win Win Win Win Win Win Win Win Win **Record**65-3 65-2 64-2 63-2 62-2 61-2 60-2 59-2 58-2 57-2 57-1 56-1 55-1 54-1 53-1 52-1 51-1 50-1 49-1 48-1 47-1 46-1 45-1 44-1 43-1 42-1 41-1 40-1 39-1 38-1 37-1 36-1 35-1 34-1 33-1 32-1 31-1 30-1 29-1 28-1 27-1 26-1 25-1 24-1 23-1 23-0 22-0 21-0 20-0 19-0 18-0 17-0 16-0 15-0 14-0 13-0 12-0 11-0 10-0 9-0 8-0 7-0 6-0 5-0 4-0 3-0 2-0 1-0 **Opponent** ▬ Rocky Marciano ▬ Jimmy Bivins ▬ Cesar Brion ▬ Lee Savold ▬ Omelio Agramonte ▬ Andy Walker ▬ Omelio Agramonte ▬ Freddie Beshore ▬ Cesar Brion ▬ Ezzard Charles ▬ Jersey Joe Walcott ▬ Jersey Joe Walcott ▬ Tami Mauriello ▬ Billy Conn ▬ Johnny Davis ▬ Abe Simon ▬ Buddy Baer ▬ Lou Nova ▬ Billy Conn ▬ Buddy Baer ▬ Tony Musto ▬ Abe Simon ▬ Gus Dorazio ▬ Clarence "Red" Burman ▬ Al McCoy ▬ Arturo Godoy ▬ Johnny Paychek ▬ Arturo Godoy ▬ Bob Pastor ▬ Tony Galento ▬ Jack Roper ▬ John Henry Lewis Max Schmeling ▬ Harry Thomas (Hermann "Harry" Pontius) ▬ Nathan Mann ▬ Tommy Farr ▬ James J. Braddock ▬ Natie Brown ▬ Bob Pastor ▬ Steve Ketchel ▬ Eddie Simms ▬ Jorge Brescia ▬ Al Ettore ▬ Jack Sharkey Max Schmeling ▬ Charley Retzlaff ▬ Paulino Uzcudun ▬ Max Baer ▬ King Levinsky ▬ Primo Carnera ▬ Roy Lazer ▬ Natie Brown ▬ Don Barry ▬ Lee Ramage Hans Birkie ▬ Patsy Perroni ▬ Lee Ramage ▬ Charley Massera ▬ Stanley Poreda ▬ Jack O'Dowd ▬ Art Sykes ▬ Adolph Wiater ▬ Al Borchuk ▬ Buck Everett ▬ Jack Kranz ▬ Larry Udell ▬ Willie Davies ▬ Jack Kracken**Type**KO Decision (unan.)Decision (unan.)KO Decision (unan.)TKO Decision (unan.)TKO Decision (unan.)Decision (unan.)KO Decision (split)KO KO TKO TKO KO TKO KO Disqualification TKO TKO KO KO TKO TKO TKO Decision (split)KO TKO KO KO KO KO KO Decision (unan.)KO KO Decision (unan.)KO TKO KO KO KO KO KO TKO KO TKO TKO KO Decision (unan.)TKO TKO TKO Decision TKO KO KO KO KO Decision TKO KO Decision TKO KO KO **Rd., Time**8 (10)10 (10)10 (10)6 (15), 2:29 10 (10)10 (10), 1:49 10 (10)4 (10), 2:48 10 (10)15 (15)11 (15)15 (15)1 (15), 2:09 8 (15), 2:19 1 (4), 0:53 6 (15)1 (15), 2:56 6 (15), 2:59 13 (15), 2:58 7 (15)9 (15), 1:36 13 (20), 1:20 2 (15), 1:30 5 (15), 2:49 6 (15)8 (15), 1:24 2 (15), 0:41 15 (15)11 (20)4 (15), 2:29 1 (10), 2:20 1 (15), 2:29 1 (15), 2:04 5 (15), 2:50 3 (15), 1:56 15 (15)8 (15)4 (10)10 (10)2 (4), 0:31 1 (10), 0:26 3 (10), 2:12 5 (15), 1:28 3 (10), 1:02 12 (15), 2:29 1 (15), 1:25 4 (15), 2:32 4 (15)1 (10), 2:21 6 (15), 2:32 3 (10), 2:26 10 (10)3 (10)2 (10), 2:11 10 (10), 1:47 10 (10)8 (10), 2:51 3 (10)1 (10), 2:40 2 (10)8 (10)10 (10)4 (10)2 (8)8 (8)2 (8)3 (6)1 (6)**Date**1951-10-26 1951-08-15 1951-08-01 1951-06-15 1951-05-02 1951-02-23 1951-02-07 1951-01-03 1950-11-29 1950-09-27 1948-06-25 1947-12-05 1946-09-18 1946-06-19 1944-11-14 1942-03-27 1942-01-09 1941-09-29 1941-06-18 1941-05-23 1941-04-08 1941-03-21 1941-02-17 1941-01-31 1940-12-16 1940-06-20 1940-03-29 1940-02-09 1939-09-20 1939-06-28 1939-04-17 1939-01-25 1938-06-22 1938-04-01 1938-02-23 1937-08-30 1937-06-22 1937-02-17 1937-01-29 1937-01-11 1936-12-14 1936-10-09

1936-09-22 1936-08-18 1936-06-19 1936-01-17 1935-12-13 1935-09-24 1935-08-07 1935-06-25
1935-04-12 1935-03-29 1935-03-08 1935-02-21 1935-01-11 1935-01-04 1934-12-14 1934-11-30
1934-11-14 1934-10-31 1934-10-24 1934-09-26 1934-09-11 1934-08-27 1934-08-13 1934-07-30
1934-07-12 1934-07-04 **Location**Madison Square Garden, New York Baltimore, MarylandSan Francisco, California Madison Square Garden, New York Detroit, Michigan San Francisco, CaliforniaMiami, FloridaDetroit, Michigan Chicago, Illinois Yankee Stadium, New York Yankee Stadium, New York Madison Square Garden, New York Yankee Stadium, New York Yankee Stadium, New York Buffalo, New York Madison Square Garden, New York Madison Square Garden, New York New York City New York City Washington, D.C.Saint Louis, MissouriDetroit, Michigan Philadelphia, Pennsylvania Madison Square Garden, New York Boston, MassachusettsYankee Stadium, New York Madison Square Garden, New York Madison Square Garden, New York Detroit, Michigan Yankee Stadium, New York Wrigley Field, Los Angeles Madison Square Garden, New York Yankee Stadium, New York Chicago, Illinois Madison Square Garden, New York Yankee Stadium, New York Chicago, Illinois Kansas City, Missouri Madison Square Garden, New York City Buffalo, New YorkCleveland, OhioHippodrome, New York City Municipal Stadium, Philadelphia Yankee Stadium, New York Yankee Stadium, New York City Chicago, Illinois Madison Square Garden, New York CityYankee Stadium, New York Chicago, Illinois Yankee Stadium, New YorkChicago, Illinois Detroit, Michigan San Francisco, California Los Angeles, California Pittsburgh, Pennsylvania Chicago, Illinois Chicago, Illinois Chicago, Illinois Chicago, Illinois Detroit, Michigan Chicago, Illinois Chicago, Illinois Detroit, MichiganChicago, Illinois Chicago, Illinois Chicago, Illinois Chicago, Illinois Chicago, Illinois**Notes**Fight was for World Heavyweight titleRetained World Heavyweight title;

Louis retired and relinquished

the title on March 1, 1949Retained World Heavyweight titleRetained World Heavyweight titleRetained World Heavyweight titleHeavyweight title at stake

per New York State Athletic Commission rulingRetained World Heavyweight titleWon World heavyweight titles of:

New York State Athletic Commission (recognized June 30, 1937)

National Boxing Association (recoginzed July 1, 1937)Opponent also known as Al Delaney

Cultural references

- In his heyday, Louis was the subject of many musical tributes, including a number of blues songs.
- Louis played a boxer in the 1938 race film *Spirit of Youth*.
- In the 1988 movie *Coming to America*, Eddie Murphy's character Clarence states that Frank Sinatra once told him that Joe Louis was 137 years old, supposedly his age when he lost to Rocky Marciano.
- Louis is also mentioned in the song "Save me Joe Louis" by Curtis Eller's American Circus from the album *Wirewalkers and Assassins*.
- Louis is played by actor Bari K. Willerford in the film *American Gangster*.
- In 2009, the Brooklyn band Yeasayer debuted the single "Ambling Alp" from their forthcoming album *Odd Blood*. The song makes reference to Louis' boxing career and his famous rivalry with Schmeling in the first person, with the lyrics such as "Oh, Max Schmeling was a formidable foe / The Ambling Alp was too, at least that's what I'm told / But if you learn one thing, you've learned it well / It's true, you must give fascists hell."
- An opera based on his life, *Shadowboxer*, premiered on 17 April 2010.

See also

- List of heavyweight boxing champions
- Joe Louis Arena (located in Detroit, Michigan)

References

- Astor, Gerald (1974). *"... And a Credit to His Race": The Hard Life and Times of Joseph Louis Barrow, a.k.a. Joe Louis*. New York: Saturday Review Press. ISBN 9780841503472.
- Bak, Richard (1998). *Joe Louis: The Great Black Hope* [2]. New York: Perseus Publishing. ISBN 9780306808791.
- Erenberg, Lewis A. (2005). *The Greatest Fight of Our Generation: Louis v. Schmeling* [3]. New York: Oxford University Press. ISBN 9780195177749.
- Gibson, Truman K.; Steve Huntley (2005). *Knocking Down Barriers: My Fight for Black America* [4]. Chicago: Northwestern University Press. ISBN 9780810122925.
- Libby, Bill (1980). *Joe Louis, the Brown Bomber*. New York: Lothrop, Lee & Shepard Books. ISBN 9780688419684.
- Louis, Joe; Edna Rust and Art Rust, Jr. (1978). *My Life*. Brighton: Angus & Robertson. ISBN 9780207958342.
- Louis, Joe; Barbara Munder (1988). *Joe Louis: 50 Years an American Hero*. New York: McGraw-Hill. ISBN 9780070039551.

- Margolick, David (2005). *Beyond Glory: Joe Louis Vs. Max Schmeling, and a World on the Brink.* New York: Vintage Books. ISBN 9780375726194.
- Mead, Chris (1985). *Champion - Joe Louis, Black Hero in White America.* New York: Scribner. ISBN 9780684184623.
- Myler, Patrick (2005). *Ring of Hate: Joe Louis vs. Max Schmeling: The Fight of the Century* [5]. New York: Arcade Publishing. ISBN 9781559707893.
- Nagler, Barney (1972). *Brown Bomber.* New York: World. ISBN 9780529045225.
- Roberts, James B.; Alexander B. Skutt (2006). *The Boxing Register: International Boxing Hall of Fame Official Record Book (4th ed.)* [6]. Ithaca: McBooks Press. ISBN 9781590131213.
- Schaap, Jeremy (2005). *Cinderella Man* [7]. Boston: Houghton Mifflin Harcourt. ISBN 9780618551170.
- Vitale, Rugio (1991). *Joe Louis: Boxing Champion* [8]. Los Angeles: Holloway House Publishing Company. ISBN 9780870675706.

This article incorporates material from the Citizendium article "Joe Louis", which is licensed under the Creative Commons Attribution-ShareAlike 3.0 Unported License but not under the GFDL.

External links

- A comprehensive collection of fight highlights, 1894-present [9]
- Video of 1936 Louis-Schmeling Fight [10]
- Video of 1937 Louis-Braddock Title Fight [11]
- Video of 1939 Louis-Galento Fight [12]
- Video of 1941 Louis-Baer Fight [13]
- Video of 1941 Louis-Conn Title Fight [14]
- Video of 1951 Louis-Charles Fight [15]
- Video of 1951 Louis-Marciano Fight [16]
- Professional boxing record for Joe Louis [17] from BoxRec
- The Fight of the Century [18] NPR special on the selection of the radio broadcast to the National Recording Registry
- Joe Louis [19] at the Internet Movie Database
- "Remembering Joe Louis" [20], WTVM
- "Joe Louis" [21]. Find a Grave. Retrieved 2008-02-07.
- http://news.google.com/newspapers?nid=897&dat=19380330&id=BjcxAAAAIBAJ&sjid=LVADAAAAIBAJ&pg=6394,4280484

Joey Maxim

Statistics	
Real name	Giuseppe Antonio Berardinelli
Rated at	Light heavyweight
Height	6 ft 1 in (1.85 m)
Reach	$72\frac{1}{2}$ in (184 cm)
Nationality	American
Birth date	March 28, 1922
Birth place	Cleveland, Ohio, U.S.
Death date	June 2, 2001 (aged 79)
Death place	West Palm Beach, Florida, U.S.
Stance	Orthodox
Boxing record	
Total fights	115
Wins	82
Wins by KO	21
Losses	29
Draws	4
No contests	0

Giuseppe Antonio Berardinelli (March 28, 1922 – June 2, 2001) was an American boxer. He was a light heavyweight champion of the world. He took the ring-name **Joey Maxim** from the Maxim gun, the world's first self-acting machine gun, based on his ability to rapidly throw a large number of left jabs.

Early career

Maxim was born in Cleveland, Ohio, he learned to box at a very young age. Following a successful amateur career, during which he won the Golden Gloves, he turned professional in 1940. He boxed fairly regularly at exhibitions during the war years whilst serving as a military police officer at Miami Beach, Florida.

Maxim becomes world champion

It is somewhat surprising that Maxim had to wait so long for a world title shot, he was 28 and had already fought 87 times as a professional, considering his undoubted ability. His chance came on January 24, 1950, against British boxer Freddie Mills, who was making his first defense, at London's Earl's Court Exhibition Centre. Maxim, very much the underdog against the popular Englishman, won the fight by knockout in the 10th round. After the fight three of Mills's teeth were found embedded in Maxim's left glove, Mills never fought again.

Maxim's next major fight was on May 30, 1951, when he made a bid for Ezzard Charles's world heavyweight title. Maxim was unsuccessful, losing on points.

June 25 1952: Joey Maxim vs. Sugar Ray Robinson

The most famous fight of Maxim's career was on June 25, 1952, when he made his second defense of his light heavyweight crown, against Sugar Ray Robinson at Yankee Stadium. The fight had originally been scheduled for June 23, but was postponed due to torrential rain. By the time the fight took place New York was in the midst of a record heat wave.

During the fight Robinson built up a large points lead over the champion, although Maxim began to come on later in the fight. Robinson gradually succumbed to hyperthermia and Maxim's harder punches. He collapsed to the canvas at the end of the 13th round, but managed to stagger back to his corner. However, Robinson failed to answer the bell at the start of the 14th, even though he only had to remain on his feet to win the fight and Maxim won by a technical knockout. This was the only time that Robinson was stopped in his 201-fight career.

By this time the original referee, Ruby Goldstein, had himself been forced to retire from the fight after collapsing into the ropes complaining that he could no longer continue. This meant that a substitute referee, Ray Miller, had to be called out to finish to fight. Goldstein and Robinson were not the only people who had to be stretchered from the stadium: several dozen spectators also collapsed during the fight. Between them, the two fighters lost over 20 pounds in weight during the fight.

Late career

Despite winning, the Robinson fight took a heavy toll on Maxim. He lost his world title six months later to the veteran Archie Moore. Following this loss Maxim, formerly one of the division's most active fighters, fought only 14 fights in the remaining 6 years of his career. These fights included two rematches with "The Old Mongoose" Archie Moore, both of which Maxim lost. Maxim retired in 1958 after losing six consecutive fights.

Maxim retired with a record of 82 wins (21 by KO), 29 losses, and 4 draws in his 115 fight career, he was knocked out only once. During his career he defeated such legendary figures as Jersey Joe Walcott, Jimmy Bivins, and Floyd Patterson.

Life after boxing

After his retirement Maxim spent time as a stand-up comic, restaurateur, taxi driver and a film extra. He was inducted into the International Boxing Hall of Fame in 1994.

External links

- Professional boxing record for Joey Maxim [1] from BoxRec
- International Boxing Hall of Fame biography [2]

Rex Layne

Rex Layne was born in Lewiston, Utah on June 7, 1928. He died on June 7, 2000

Background

According to the Oct. 29, 1949 Tacoma News Tribune, Layne was a Mormon who was a staff sergeant with an airborne division in World War II for 19 months, serving some time in Japan. He did not start boxing until he joined the Army. "When they sent out a call for boxing candidates at Soporo, Japan, he won the heavyweight championship of our troops in Nippon. Returning home in 1947, he dropped a close decision in an Olympic tryout to Jay Lambert, who won the United States Olympic title, and lost a decision in the London semifinals. Last spring Layne lost a close verdict to Utah

Rex Layne (r.) fighting with Heinz Neuhaus

State's Dale Panter in the Utah Golden Gloves, but earned a trip to Boston acquiring the A.A.U. Intermountain amateur championship by a knockout. In the Hub he won four bouts, three by knockouts, to account for the national championship."

Amateur career

Rex Layne was a Salt Lake City sugar beet farmer when he won the 1949 National AAU Heavyweight Championship.

Professional career

His final record stands at 50-17-3 (34 KO). He was undefeated his first 17 fights.

He fought legendary boxer Rocky Marciano and lost by 6th round KO. Marciano's knockout punch sheared off four of Layne's upper, front teeth at the gumline and sent his mouthpiece ten feet across the ring.

Trivia

- Was Featured on the cover of the May 1951 The Ring magazine.

His outstanding career featured wins over such champions as Ezzard Charles and Joe Walcott, as well as other notable contenders such as Bob Satterfield.

References

- Professional boxing record for Rex Layne [1] from BoxRec

External links

- Video of Layne's loss to Rocky Marciano [2]

Coley Wallace

Coley Wallace (April 5, 1927-January 30, 2005) was an American actor and heavyweight boxer who ^was outpointed by Rocky Marciano in a three-round amateur fight.

Although Wallace, a Jacksonville, FL native had a respectable record as a professional (20-7-0), his claim to fame came in 1948 when, as an amateur, he was defeated by future heavyweight champion Rocky Marciano in the finals of the New York Golden Gloves Tournament.

After boxing, Wallace acted in four movies, twice portraying the boxer Joe Louis.

Wallace died on January 30, 2005, of heart failure in New York City.

Filmography

- *The Joe Louis Story* (1953) - Joe Louis
- *Carib Gold* (1957)
- *Raging Bull* (1980) - Joe Louis (Cerdan Fight)
- *Rooftops* (1989) - Lester

External links

- Professional boxing record for Coley Wallace [1] from BoxRec
- Wallace IMDB.com Page [2]

Bob Satterfield

Bob "Bombardier" Satterfield (November 9, 1923 in St. Louis, MO – June 1, 1977), was a heavyweight boxer who fought from 1945-1957. Satterfield, who never fought for the title, retired with a record of 50 wins (35 KOs), 25 losses and 4 draws. He is in Ring magazine's list of 100 greatest punchers of all time at number 58. Satterfield later died from cancer at the age of 53.

Amateur career

Satterfield was the Chicago City Golden Gloves 147-pound champion in 1941.

Professional career

Satterfield, known for his punching power and aggressive style, was a fan favorite. His poor stamina and weak chin often cost him fights, however. In his bout against heavyweight contender Rex Layne on March 9, 1951, Satterfield hurt Layne, and knocked him down for an eight count in the first round. Layne slowly retook control of the fight, and ultimately knocked out Satterfield in the eighth round.

Satterfield was knocked out in 7 rounds by future middleweight champion Jake LaMotta on September 12, 1946. He was also knocked out in 2 rounds by former heavyweight champion Ezzard Charles on January 13, 1954. Satterfield did score a knockout over heavyweight contender Cleveland Williams and also beat the dangerous giant Cuban Nino Valdes, but lost by KO to light heavyweight champion Archie Moore, and dropped 2 out of 3 to future light heavyweight champion Harold Johnson.

In the media

The 2007 motion picture *Resurrecting the Champ* is based on an *L.A. Times Magazine* article about a reporter named Erik Kernan Jr. who finds a homeless man claiming to be Bob Satterfield and writes an article about him in the *Denver Times Magazine*. The film stars Samuel L. Jackson, Josh Hartnett and Alan Alda and was directed by Rod Lurie.

Trivia

- Satterfield served in the United States Army from 1942-45.
- It has been reported that he was friends with musician Miles Davis and introduced Muhammad Ali to his first wife.

External links

- Video of Knockout win over Bob Baker [1]
- Professional boxing record for Bob Satterfield [2] from BoxRec

Rocky Marciano

Statistics	
Real name	Rocco Francis Marchegiano
Nickname(s)	The Brockton Blockbuster The Rock from Brockton
Rated at	Heavyweight
Height	5 ft 10 in (1.78 m)
Reach	67 in (170 cm)
Nationality	American
Birth date	September 1, 1923
Birth place	Brockton, Massachusetts
Death date	August 31, 1969 (aged 45)
Death place	Near Newton, Iowa
Stance	Orthodox
Boxing record	
Total fights	49
Wins	49
Wins by KO	43
Losses	0
Draws	0
No contests	0

Rocky Marciano (September 1, 1923 – August 31, 1969), born Rocco Francis Marchegiano, was an Italian-American boxer and the heavyweight champion of the world from September 23, 1952, to April 27, 1956. When he retired he became the only heavyweight champion to finish his career undefeated. Remembered for notable victories against Joe Louis, Jersey Joe Walcott, Roland La Starza, Ezzard Charles and Archie Moore. He is considered one of the greatest boxers of all time.

Early years

Marciano was an Italian-American, born and raised in Brockton, Massachusetts to Pierino Marchegiano and Pasqualina Picciuto. Both of his parents were immigrants from Italy: his father was from Ripa Teatina, Abruzzo, while his mother was from San Bartolomeo in Galdo, Campania. Rocky had three sisters—Alice, Concetta, and Elizabeth—and two brothers—Sonny and Peter. When he was about eighteen months old, he contracted pneumonia, from which he almost died.

In his youth, he played baseball, worked out on homemade weightlifting equipment, and used a stuffed mail bag that hung from a tree in his back yard as a heavy bag. He attended Brockton High School, where he played on the American football and baseball teams. However, he was cut from the school baseball team because he had joined a church league, violating a school rule forbidding players from joining other teams. He dropped out of school after finishing tenth grade.

Marciano then worked as a chute man on delivery trucks for the Brockton Ice and Coal Company. He also worked as a ditch digger and as a shoemaker. Rocky was also a resident of Hanson, Massachusetts; the house he lived in still stands on Main Street.

In March 1943, Marciano was drafted into the Army for a term of two years. Stationed in Swansea, Wales, he helped ferry supplies across the English Channel to Normandy. After the war ended, he completed his service in March 1946 at Fort Lewis, Washington.

Amateur circuit

While awaiting discharge, Marciano, representing the army, won the 1946 amateur armed forces boxing tournament. His amateur career was interrupted on March 17, 1947, when Marciano stepped into the ring as a professional competitor. That night, he knocked out Lee Epperson in three rounds. In an unusual move, however, Marciano returned to the amateur ranks and fought in the Golden Gloves All-East Championship Tournament in March 1948. He was beaten by Coley Wallace. He continued to fight as an amateur throughout the spring and competed in the AAU Olympic tryouts in the Boston Garden. There, he knocked out George McInnis, but hurt his hands during the bout and was forced to withdraw from the tournament. That was his last amateur bout. His amateur years, with an 8-4 record, would be the last time Marciano experienced a loss.

In late March, 1947, Marciano and a few of his friends traveled to Fayetteville, North Carolina, to try out for the Fayetteville Cubs, a farm team for the Chicago Cubs baseball team. Marciano lasted three weeks before being cut. After failing to find a spot on another team, he returned to Brockton and began boxing training with longtime friend, Allie Colombo. Al Weill served as his manager and Charley Goldman as his trainer and teacher.

Professional career

Although he had one professional fight (against Lee Epperson) on his record, Marciano began fighting permanently as a professional boxer on July 12, 1948. That night, he notched a win over Harry Bilizarian. He won his first sixteen bouts by knockout, all before the fifth round, and nine before the first round was over. Don Mogard became the first boxer to last the distance (full 10 rounds scheduled) with "The Rock," but Marciano won by decision.

Early in his career, he changed the spelling of his last name. The ring announcer in Providence, Rhode Island could not pronounce Marchegiano, so Marciano's handler, Al Weill, suggested they create a pseudonym. The first suggestion was Rocky Mack, which Marciano rejected. He decided to go with the more Italian-sounding "Marciano".

Marciano won three more fights by knockout, and then he met Ted Lowry, who, according to many scribes and witnesses, probably managed to win three or four of the ten rounds from Marciano. Nevertheless, Marciano kept his winning streak alive by beating Lowry by decision. Marciano fought Lowry again in November 1950 and it too went the scheduled ten round distance. Four more knockout wins followed his first fight with Lowry, including a five rounder on December 19, 1949 with Phil Muscato, an experienced heavyweight from Buffalo, New York, and the first "name fighter" Marciano would face. Three weeks after that fight, Marciano beat Carmine Vingo in a fifth round knockout in New York that almost killed Vingo. When Marciano next fought in late March 1950, he gained a hard-fought ten-round decision victory over the fighter who would later become his 1953 world title challenger, Roland La Starza. The victory over La Starza was extremely close.

Marciano won three more knockouts in a row before a rematch with Lowry. Marciano again won, by unanimous decision. After that, he won four more by knockout, and, after a decision win over Red Applegate late April 1951, he was showcased on national television for the first time, when he knocked out Rex Layne in six rounds on July 12, 1951. One more win, and he was again on national TV, this time against Joe Louis. Marciano defeated Louis in what would be the latter's last career bout, a result that left him with mixed emotions, as Louis had been his childhood idol.

Championship

After four more wins, including victories over Lee Savold and Harry Matthews, Marciano faced the world heavyweight champion, 38-year-old Jersey Joe Walcott, in Philadelphia on September 23, 1952. Walcott dropped Marciano in the first round and steadily built a points lead; but in the thirteenth, Marciano's "Suzie Q" right cross knocked Walcott unconscious, and Marciano was the new world heavyweight champion. His first defense came a year later against Walcott, who this time was knocked out in the first round. Next, it was Roland La Starza's turn to challenge Marciano. After building a small lead on the judges' scorecards all the way to the middle rounds, Marciano won by a technical knockout in the eleventh round.

Then came two consecutive bouts against former world heavyweight champion and light-heavyweight legend Ezzard Charles, who became the only man to ever last fifteen rounds against Marciano. Marciano won the first fight on points and the second by an eighth-round knockout. Then, Marciano met British and European champion, Don Cockell. Marciano knocked him out in the ninth.

Marciano's last title bout was against Archie Moore on September 21, 1955. The bout was originally scheduled for September 20, but because of hurricane warnings, it had to be delayed a day. Marciano was knocked down for a four count in the second round. Marciano recovered, and retained his title by way of a KO in round nine.

Marciano announced his retirement on April 27, 1956.

After boxing

Marciano considered a comeback in 1959 when Ingemar Johansson won the heavyweight championship from Floyd Patterson on June 26, 1959. After only a month of training in three years, Marciano decided against it and never seriously considered a comeback again.

After his retirement, Marciano entered the world of television, first appearing in the "Combat!" episode "Masquerade", and then hosting a weekly boxing show on TV in 1961. For a brief period, he worked as a troubleshooting referee in wrestling (Marciano was a good wrestler in high school). He continued as a referee and boxing commentator in boxing matches for many years. He was also active in business as a partner and vice president of Papa Luigi Spaghetti Dens, a San Francisco based franchise company formed by Joe Kearns and James Braly.

In late July 1969, shortly before his death, Marciano participated in the filming of the fantasy, *The Superfight: Marciano vs. Ali.* The two boxers were filmed sparring, then the film was edited to match a computer simulation of a hypothetical fight between them, each in their prime. It aired on January 20, 1970, with Marciano winning by knockout in round 13 in North American theatres and Ali winning in European theatres.

Death

In 1969, on the eve of his 46th birthday, Marciano was a passenger in a small private plane, a Cessna 172 headed to Des Moines, Iowa. It was at night, and bad weather set in. The pilot, Glenn Belz, had only 231 total hours of flying time, only 35 of them at night, and was not certified to fly in Instrument Meteorological Conditions. Belz tried to set the plane down at a small airfield outside Newton, Iowa, but hit a tree two miles short of the runway. Rocky, Belz (the young pilot), and 22 year old Frankie Farrell (son of Italian mobster Louis Fratto) were killed on impact. The National Transportation Safety Board report said, "The pilot attempted operation exceeding his experience and ability level, continued visual flight rules under adverse weather conditions, and experienced spatial disorientation in the last moments of the flight." . Marciano was on his way to give a speech to support a friend's son and there was a surprise birthday celebration waiting for him. He had hoped to return early morning for his 46th birthday celebration with his wife. He was coming from a dinner in Chicago at STP CEO Andy Granatelli's home.

He is interred in a crypt at Forest Lawn Memorial Cemetery in Fort Lauderdale, Florida. His wife, who died five years after him at the age of 46, is entombed next to him. His father died in March 1972, his mother in early January 1986.

Legacy

In 1971, Ring magazine founder Nat Fleischer named Marciano as the tenth greatest heavyweight champion ever. In 1998, Ring magazine named Marciano as the sixth greatest heavyweight champion ever. In 2002, Ring Magazine numbered Marciano at #12 on the list of the 80 Best Fighters of the Last 80 Years. In 2003, Ring Magazine rated Marciano #14 on the list of 100 greatest punchers of all time. In 2005, Marciano was named the fifth greatest heavyweight of all time by the International Boxing Research Organization. A 1977 ranking by Ring magazine listed Marciano as the greatest Italian-American fighter. In 2007, on ESPN.com's list of the 50 Greatest Boxers of All Time, Marciano was ranked #14. A 1968 radio computer simulation by Murry Woroner concluded that Marciano was the greatest heavyweight champion.

Marciano holds the record for the longest undefeated streak by a heavyweight and for being the only world heavyweight champion to go undefeated throughout his career. This record was challenged by Larry Holmes in 1985 when Holmes went 48-0 before losing to Michael Spinks twice. Light heavyweight Dariusz Michalczewski also challenged Marciano's record when he was 48-0, but lost to Julio César González in his 49th fight. Julio César Chávez holds the record for longest win streak with eighty-eight straight until he suffered a draw in 1993. Heavyweight Brian Nielsen tied Marciano's record but lost his 50th fight against Dicky Ryan.Willie Pep, a featherweight, had a perfect 62-0 record before he was defeated once, followed by a 72-0-1 undefeated streak. Packy McFarland was a lightweight (fighting between 1904–1915) who lost his first fight and then won his next 98, though he never won the lightweight title.

Throughout history, only a few boxers have retired as undefeated world champions. As of 2009 apart from Marciano only Michael Loewe, Pichit Sitbangprachan, Harry Simon, Sven Ottke and Joe Calzaghe retired with a perfect record containing neither defeats nor draws. Ji Won Kim, Terry Marsh and Ricardo Lopez retired without losing a fight but having had at least one draw on their record. Edwin Valero's career ended with his death when he had a 27-0 record.

Marciano was knocked down to the canvas only twice in his professional career. The first occurred in his first championship against Jersey Joe Walcott and the second occurred against Archie Moore. On both occasions, he rose to knock his opponent out. Moore stated, after the fight, that fighting Marciano was "like fighting an airplane propeller."

Marciano's punch was tested and it was featured in the December 1963 issue of *Boxing Illustrated*: "Marciano's knockout blow packs more explosive energy than an armour-piercing bullet and represents as much energy as would be required to spot lift 1000 pounds one foot off the ground."

Marciano was named fighter of the year by *Ring Magazine* three times. His three championship fights between 1952-54 were named fights of the year by that magazine. In 2006, an ESPN poll voted Marciano's 1952 championship bout against Walcott as the greatest knockout ever. Marciano also received the Hickok Belt for top professional athlete of the year in 1952. In 1955, he was voted second most important American athlete of the year.

Marciano is a member of the International Boxing Hall Of Fame.

A bronze statue of Marciano is planned for 2009 in his hometown of Brockton, MA. The statue will be made a gift to the city by the World Boxing Council. A location for the statue has yet to be decided. The artist Mario Rendon, head of the Instituto Universitario de las Bellas Artes in Colima, Mexico, has been selected to sculpt the statue.

Professional boxing record

49 Wins (43 knockouts, 6 decisions), 0 Losses, 0 Draws						
Result	Opponent	Type	Rd., Time	Date	Location	Notes
Win	Archie Moore	KO	9 (15), 1:19	1955-09-21	The Bronx, NY	Retained World Heavyweight title. After the fight he would retire on 1956-04-27.
Win	Don Cockell	KO	9 (15), 0:54	1955-05-16	San Francisco, CA	Retained World Heavyweight title.
Win	Ezzard Charles	KO	8 (15)	1954-09-17	The Bronx, NY	Retained World Heavyweight title.
Win	Ezzard Charles	Decision (unanimous)	(15)	1954-06-17	The Bronx, NY	Retained World Heavyweight title.
Win	Roland La Starza	TKO	11 (15)	1953-09-24	New York City, NY	Retained World Heavyweight title.
Win	Jersey Joe Walcott	KO	1 (15), 2:25	1953-05-15	Chicago, IL	Retained World Heavyweight title.
Win	Jersey Joe Walcott	KO	13 (15), 0:43	1952-09-23	Philadelphia, PA	Won World Heavyweight title.

Win	Harry Matthews	KO	2 (10), 2:04	1952-07-28	The Bronx, NY	
Win	Bernie Reynolds	KO	3 (10), 2:21	1952-05-12	Providence, RI	
Win	Gino Buonvino	KO	2 (10)	1952-04-21	Providence, RI	
Win	Lee Savold	KO	6 (10), 0:00	1952-02-13	Philadelphia, PA	
Win	Joe Louis	KO	8 (10)	1951-10-26	New York City, NY	
Win	Freddie Beshore	KO	4 (10), 0:50	1951-08-27	Boston, MA	
Win	Rex Layne	KO	6 (10), 0:35	1951-07-12	New York City, NY	
Win	Red Applegate	Decision (unanimous)	10 (10)	1951-04-30	Providence, RI	
Win	Art Henri	TKO	9 (10), 2:51	1951-03-26	Providence, RI	
Win	Harold Mitchell	KO	2 (10), 2:45	1951-03-20	Hartford, CT	
Win	Keene Simmons	KO	8 (10), 2:54	1951-01-29	Providence, RI	
Win	Bill Wilson	KO	1 (10), 1:50	1950-12-18	Providence, RI	
Win	Ted Lowry	Decision (unanimous)	10 (10)	1950-11-13	Providence, RI	
Win	Johnny Shkor	KO	6 (10), 1:28	1950-09-18	Providence, RI	
Win	Gino Buonvino	KO	10 (10), 0:25	1950-07-10	Boston, MA	
Win	Eldridge Eatman	KO	3 (10)	1950-06-05	Providence, RI	
Win	Roland La Starza	Decision (split decision)	10 (10)	1950-03-24	New York City, NY	
Win	Carmine Vingo	KO	6 (10)	1949-12-30	New York City, NY	

Win	Phil Muscato	KO	5 (10), 1:15	1949-12-19	Providence, RI	
Win	Pat Richards	KO	2 (10), 0:39	1949-12-02	New York City, NY	
Win	Joe Dominic	KO	2 (10), 2:26	1949-11-07	Providence, RI	
Win	Ted Lowry	Decision (unanimous)	10 (10)	1949-10-10	Providence, RI	
Win	Tommy DiGiorgio	KO	4 (10), 2:54	1949-09-26	Providence, RI	
Win	Pete Louthis	KO	3 (10)	1949-08-16	New Bedford, MA	
Win	Harry Haft	KO	3 (10), 2:21	1949-07-18	Providence, RI	
Win	Don Mogard	Decision	10 (10)	1949-05-23	Providence, RI	
Win	Jimmy Evans	KO	3 (10)	1949-05-02	Providence, RI	
Win	Jimmy Walls	KO	3 (10), 2:54	1949-04-14	Providence, RI	
Win	Artie Donato	KO	1 (10), 0:33	1949-03-28	Providence, RI	
Win	Johnny Pretzie	KO	5 (10), 1:46	1949-03-21	Providence, RI	
Win	Gilley Ferron	KO	2 (6), 2:21	1948-12-14	Philadelphia, PA	
Win	James Connolly	KO	1 (8), 0:57	1948-11-29	Providence, RI	
Win	Bob Jefferson	KO	2 (6), 2:30	1948-10-04	Providence, RI	
Win	Gilbert Cardone	KO	1 (4), 0:36	1948-09-30	Providence, RI	
Win	Bill Hardeman	KO	1 (6)	1948-09-20	Providence, RI	
Win	Jerry Jackson	KO	1 (6), 1:08	1948-09-13	Providence, RI	
Win	Jimmy Weeks	KO	1 (6), 2:50	1948-08-30	Providence, RI	

Win	Eddie Ross	KO	1 (6), 1:03	1948-08-23	Providence, RI	
Win	Bobby Quinn	KO	3 (4), 0:22	1948-08-09	Providence, RI	
Win	John Edwards	KO	1 (4), 1:19	1948-07-19	Providence, RI	
Win	Harry Bilzerian	KO	1 (4)	1948-07-12	Providence, RI	
Win	Lee Epperson	KO	3 (4)	1947-03-17	Holyoke, MA	

See also

- List of heavyweight boxing champions

References and notes

External links

- Professional boxing record for Rocky Marciano [1] from BoxRec
- Rocky Marciano [2] at Find a Grave
- Rocky Marciano // Official Website [3]
- Check-Six.com - The Crash of Rocky Marciano's Cessna plane [4]
- *Rocky Marciano* [5] at the Internet Movie Database
- ESPN Greatest Ever KO Poll [6]
- Marciano feature from SPORT magazine [7]

The distance (boxing)

The distance, in boxing, refers to the full number of rounds in boxing matches. It is frequently used in the expression "going the distance," which means fighting a full bout without being knocked out. If a match goes the distance without a knockout or other decision then it is either tied or is decided on points.

In title fights, this is called "**the championship distance**," which today usually means 12 rounds (See history section), though there were some ten-round championship matches. Non-title fights can be of any length under 12 rounds but are typically 10 rounds or fewer. Women's championship boxing is ten rounds or fewer, each round lasting 2 minutes instead of 3 for men.

History

In the early days of bare-knuckle boxing, there was no limit on the number of rounds and so matches would be fought to a conclusion (i.e. with a knockout or tap out). For example, the match between Simon Byrne and James 'Deaf' Burke in 1833 lasted 3¼ hours. Subsequently, laws and rules were passed to prevent such protracted bouts. When John L. Sullivan made boxing under Queensbury rules with gloved hands popular, his matches were of a pre-determined length and the referee would decide the winner if they went the distance. If a match reached the prescribed limit without a formal result then the result would be "no-decision", though one boxer might be considered the winner by popular acclaim—a "newspaper win." To regulate such results better, official judges were appointed to award points so that technical winner could be determined. For a period, titles in many US states could not be lost if the match went the distance.

For amateur boxing, the Amateur Boxing Association of England set rules for the length of a match when it was formed in 1880. Initially there were three rounds of 3, 3 and 4 minutes with a break of 1 minute between them. Changes were made in 1926 and 1997 and most recently, in 2000, the International Boxing Association made it four rounds of two minutes each.

Championships shortened

In professional boxing, until the 1980s, the "championship distance" generally referred to the title rounds that numbered between 13 and 15. For decades, the last heavyweight title match scheduled for less than 15 rounds had been the September 22, 1927 10-rounder between Gene Tunney and Jack Dempsey; from then, the only bout that wasn't scheduled for 15 rounds had been a *scheduled* 20-rounder between Joe Louis and Abe Simon on March 21, 1941. This changed though, following the death of lightweight Duk Koo Kim in 1982 after his fourteen-round fight with Ray Mancini, which was so shocking that two people committed suicide as a result. Almost immediately, the World Boxing Council (WBC) issued a statement saying that WBC world title bouts would be set for 12 rounds.

The following year on March 27, 1983, the first ever heavyweight title fight scheduled for 12 rounds under that rule was held by the WBC between Larry Holmes and Lucien Rodriguez. The World Boxing Association (which then included the WBO) later followed suit by voting to reduce their championship distances to 12 rounds on October 19, 1987. While the International Boxing Federation continued to hold onto the position there was no documented medical evidence to show a 15-round fight is more dangerous than a 12-round fight, they eventually voted to shorten their championship distance to 12 rounds as well on June 3, 1988.

The last heavyweight 15-rounder title fight was a rematch on April 11, 1986 between Larry Holmes and Michael Spinks.

In recent years, there have been calls to return the championship distance to 15 rounds. For example, the debate following the Bernard Hopkins-Jermain Taylor fight on July 16, 2005 questioned whether Taylor, who was "losing steam" in the later rounds, would have won the title match were it a 15-round bout.

Distance change criticisms

The shift from a 15 round to a 12 round distance for title fights has been controversial. There have been studies which show that the brain becomes more susceptible to damage after the 12th round. Moreover, it has been argued that the 15 round distance greatly increased the risk of dehydration and exhaustion.

However, "purists" of the sport have contended that the shift from 15 rounds to 12 rounds has impacted viewership of the sport. Moreover, Frank Lotierzo, a critic of the 12-round limit, pointed out that fatalities are rare in heavyweight matches, instead attributing deaths to dehydration from the pressure of "making weight" for lower weight classes:

> "In my opinion, the reason that you hardly ever see fatalities in the heavyweight division is because the big guys don't have to make weight. In many cases, fighters under 150 pounds dehydrate themselves shedding those last few pounds too [sic] make weight. This leaves them vulnerable to brain injuries with a lack a fluid around their skull protecting the brain from crashing against it when they are hit. I believe this is more of a danger than fighters fighting 15 rounds. If I'm wrong, someone please explain why we rarely see heavyweights being killed in the ring? You would think most boxing fatalities would occur in the heavyweight division since they are clearly the most powerful punchers."

Lotierzo also argues that part of the motivation for a 12-round limit was not so much for safety, but to allow the matches to appear on network television. Previously, the timing of boxing involved 15 three-minute rounds with 14 one-minute intervals between each round, the preamble, and post-fight interviews—requiring around 70–75 minutes; in contrast, a 12-round bout lasts 47 minutes, which fits neatly into a one-hour time slot when pre- and post-fight programming and commercials are added in.

Nonetheless, it has been noted that these rule changes have made certain kinds of boxing deaths far rarer, though boxing remains the 8th most deadly sport with 1.3 deaths per 100,000 participants.

Speculation regarding change

It has been argued that "some of the greatest moments in sports would never have occurred" were the 12-round limit imposed in earlier matches. Nonetheless, entirely different strategies might have been used were the fights scheduled for only 12 rather than 15 rounds, so it is possible that some or all matches could have ended the same way regardless of whether the scheduled distance were 12 or 15 rounds.

The following are some of the most notable longer championship distances, including the Fight of the Century, that would have had the reverse result were they abruptly ended after the 12th round:

- **June 18, 1941: Joe Louis vs. Billy Conn** — In this heavyweight championship match, Conn, the light-heavyweight titleholder, challenged Loius, the defending champion. Leading on all three scorecards, Conn would have captured the title were the bout only 12 rounds long, which might have prevented Louis from retaining the title by knocking out Conn with a six-punch barrage in the 13th round.

- **June 17, 1954: Rocky Marciano vs. Ezzard Charles** — For much of the match, it appeared that Charles would become the first former champion to regain the heavyweight crown. However, in each of the final rounds Marciano unleashed three-minute non-stop striking combinations, earning a close but unanimous victory over Charles. Had this been 12 rounds, Marciano would not have become, to this day, the only heavyweight champion to have finished his career undefeated. Charles also became the only man ever to last the full 15-round distance against Marciano.

- **July 13, 1966: Emile Griffith vs. Joey Archer** — Had this middleweight championship not gone the 15-round distance, the title would have been captured by Archer, but the defender outlasted and wore down Archer to retain it in the end.

- **March 8, 1971: Fight of the Century (Joe Frazier vs. Muhammad Ali)** — It has been argued that the apparent outcome of the match was reversed after "one of histories [*sic*] greatest left-hooks ever," which was thrown in the 14th round.

- **September 16, 1981: Sugar Ray Leonard vs. Thomas Hearns** — In what has been called "the biggest and most anticipated fight in welterweight history," Leonard was behind Hearns after the 12th round, though rallying to win in the 14th.

It has also been argued that various 12-rounders would have ended differently were they extended for additional rounds:

- **April 6, 1987: Marvin Hagler vs. Sugar Ray Leonard** — Before the match, it was believed that Leonard's decision to challenge Hagler, the World Middleweight Champion, was a dangerous mistake that seemed destined to result in "a brutal knockout loss." However, Leonard prevented Hagler from scoring by repeatedly dodging Hagler's heavy hits for the surprising upset victory by points. It was noted that Leonard was clearly more exhausted by the tactic than Hagler towards the final rounds and might not have been able to maintain his point lead for 15 rounds.

- **July 16, 2005: Bernard Hopkins vs. Jermain Taylor I** — The debate following the fight raised the question of whether Taylor, who was "losing steam" in the later rounds, would have won the title match were it a 15-round bout.

Popular culture

See also: Going the distance (disambiguation)

"Going the distance" was featured prominently in the 1976 film *Rocky* in which Rocky Balboa and Apollo Creed fight 15 rounds for the World Heavyweight Championship. Rocky says,

> Nobody's ever gone the distance with Creed, and if I can go that distance, you see, and that bell rings and I'm still standin', I'm gonna know for the first time in my life, see, that I weren't just another bum from the neighbourhood.

Balboa (Sylvester Stallone) and Creed (Carl Weathers) nearly go the distance again in their rematch in 1979's *Rocky II*, as do Rocky and Ivan Drago in their showdown in *Rocky IV*. Balboa's final fight against Mason "The Line" Dixon in *Rocky Balboa* lasts the maximum of 10 rounds.

Balboa's use of the term has also inspired its use in other works.

- "Go the Distance" is a song written for the Disney animated feature *Hercules* by Alan Menken, who also wrote the song "The Measure of a Man" for *Rocky V*.
- In *Command & Conquer: Yuri's Revenge*, Sylvester Stallone (voice impersonated) is featured as an in-game celebrity character, "Sammy Stallion," who frequently says, "I'm goin' the distance," when directed to move in the battlefield of the Hollywood mission.

Boxing Records

Middleweight

Middleweight is a division, or weight class, in boxing. Early boxing history is less than exact, but the middleweight designation seems to have begun in the 1840s. In the bare-knuckle era, the first middleweight championship fight was between Tom Chandler and Dooney Harris in 1867. Chandler won, becoming known as the American middleweight champion.

The first middleweight fight with gloves *may* have been between George Fulljames and Jack (Nonpareil) Dempsey (no relation to the more famous heavyweight of the same name). Dempsey knocked out Fulljames on July 30, 1884.

In the modern era, middleweight means that the fighter's official weight does not exceed 160 pounds (72.64 kg). (In practice, however, since weigh-ins take place usually 24 hours before the actual fight, many fighters show up at the actual ringside weighing more.)

The current middleweight champion, Sergio Martinez, won a U.D. victory in April 2010, defeating the defending champion, Kelly Pavlik.

Some notable middleweights have been:

- Arthur Abraham
- Fred Apostoli
- Nigel Benn, 27 KOs from 31 middleweight contests, won WBO version of title and WBC title at super-middle
- Nino Benvenuti, world champion in 1967 and again from 1968 to 1970.
- Marcel Cerdan, the first non-American to win a world middleweight title.
- Billy Conn
- Roberto Durán, The "Hands of Stone" defeated Iran Barkley for the WBC middleweight championship.
- Chris Eubank unbeaten in 28 middleweight contests, held WBO title at middle and super-middle, beat Benn.
- Bob Fitzsimmons, who was the first fighter - there have only been a handful since - to hold titles in three of the original eight divisions, and the first middleweight champion to capture the heavyweight title
- Gene Fullmer
- Ceferino Garcia,The Heaviest Filipino boxing champion
- Rocky Graziano

- Harry Greb
- "Marvelous" Marvin Hagler, defended his title 12 times, first middleweight champion to hold top three sanctioning body belts.
- Bernard Hopkins, defended his title a record 20 times, first fighter in history to unify the WBO, WBC, IBF and WBA titles
- Stanley Ketchel
- Jake "Raging Bull" LaMotta
- Sergio Martinez, current middleweight champion.
- Carlos Monzón, who unified the title and defended it 14 times
- Kelly Pavlik
- Sugar Ray Robinson, held the title a record five times. Widely considered greatest pound-for-pound boxer ever.
- Freddie Steele
- Rodrigo Valdez The only one to have knocked out Monzon and the World Champion in 1977.
- Mickey Walker
- Tony Zale
- Oscar de la Hoya Former WBO Middleweight Champion.
- Dmitry Pirog

Olympic champions

- 1904 – Charles Mayer (USA)
- 1908 – John Douglas (GBR)
- 1920 – Harry Mallin (GBR)
- 1924 – Harry Mallin (GBR)
- 1928 – Piero Toscani (ITA)
- 1932 – Carmen Barth (USA)
- 1936 – Jean Despeaux (FRA)
- 1948 – László Papp (HUN)
- 1952 – Floyd Patterson (USA)
- 1956 – Gennadiy Shatkov (URS)
- 1960 – Eddie Crook, Jr. (USA)
- 1964 – Valeriy Popenchenko (URS)
- 1968 – Chris Finnegan (GBR)
- 1972 – Vyacheslav Lemeshev (URS)
- 1976 – Michael Spinks (USA)
- 1980 – José Gómez (CUB)
- 1984 – Shin Joon-Sup (KOR)

- 1988 – ▨ Henry Maske (GDR)
- 1992 – ▤ Ariel Hernández (CUB)
- 1996 – ▤ Ariel Hernández (CUB)
- 2000 – ▤ Jorge Gutiérrez (CUB)
- 2004 – ▬ Gaydarbek Gaydarbekov (RUS)
- 2008 – ▧ James DeGale (GBR)

Professional Champions

Current champions

Sanctioning Body	Reign Began	Champion	Record	Defenses
WBA	April 28, 2007	▬ Felix Sturm	34-2-1 (14 KO)	8
WBC	April 17, 2010	▤ Sergio Gabriel Martinez	45-2-2 (24 KO)	0
IBF	September 19, 2009	▬ Sebastian Sylvester	33-3-1 (16 KO)	2
WBO	July 31, 2010	▬ Dmitry Pirog	17-0 (14 KO)	0

- List of middleweight boxing champions

Taekwondo

Category	Men's	Women's	Competitions	Note
Middleweight	78 – 84 kg	67 – 72 kg	World Championships, Continental Championships, Asian Games	since 1999
Middleweight	76 – 83 kg	65 – 70 kg	World Championships, Continental Championships, Asian Games	until 1998
Middleweight	68 – 80 kg	57 – 67 kg	Olympic Games, Pan Am Games, All-Africa Games	

Kickboxing

- International Kickboxing Federation (IKF) Middleweight (Pro & Amateur) 159.1 lbs. - 165 lbs. or 72.4 kg - 75 kg

Chicago Golden Gloves

This amateur boxing tournament is considered by many boxing aficionados as one of the three most elite Golden Gloves titles, along with the Intercity Golden Gloves and the New York Golden Gloves. The tournament is also more formally known as the Chicago Tribune Charities Golden Gloves Tournament of Champions. It was initiated by the Chicago Tribune sports editor Arch Ward in the 1920's.

History

The regional Chicago and New York Golden Gloves Championships were the two crown jewels of the boxing mecca of the United States. In 1962, with the National Golden Gloves assuming control of the tournament, with a growing televised economy, the general public's emphasis progressed more towards a national championship.

The Chicago, New York and Intercity tournaments were fought in eight weight divisions: 112 lb., 118 lb., 125 lb., 135.lb., 147 lb., 160 lb., 175 lb. and Heavyweight.

External links

- Official site [1]

World Boxing Association

The **World Boxing Association (WBA)** (Spanish: Asociacion Mundial de Boxeo) is a boxing organization that sanctions official matches, and awards the WBA world championship title at the professional level. It was previously known as the National Boxing Association before changing its name in 1962. It is the oldest of the major organizations recognized by IBHOF which sanction world championship boxing bouts, alongside the International Boxing Federation, the World Boxing Council and the World Boxing Organization.

History

The original sanctioning body of professional boxing, the World Boxing Association can be traced back to the original National Boxing Association, organized in 1921; the first bout recognized by the organization being the Jack Dempsey-Georges Carpentier Heavyweight Championship bout in New Jersey, USA.

The NBA was formed by representatives from thirteen American states to counterbalance the influence the New York State Athletic Commission (NYSAC) wielded in the boxing world. This often meant that the NBA and the NYSAC crowned different world champions in the same division, leading to confusion about who was the real champion.

The International Boxing Research Organization describes the early NBA in this way: "Originally more comparable to the present American Association of Boxing Commissions than to its offspring and successor, the NBA sanctioned title bouts, published lists of outstanding challengers, withdrew titular recognition, but did not attempt to appoint its own title bout officials or otherwise impose its will on championship fights. It also did not conduct purse bids or collect 'sanctioning fees.'"

In 1962 the NBA, with the growth of boxing's popularity worldwide, changed its name to the **World Boxing Association**. The organization remained mainly American until 1974, however. In that year, two Panamanian boxing figures named Rodrigo Sanchez and Elias Cordova manipulated the WBA rules to give a majority of votes to nations in Latin America.

Gilberto Mendoza has been the President of the WBA since 1982. The WBA in the 1990s moved its central offices from Panama City, Panama, to Caracas, Venezuela. In January 2007 it moved its offices again to Panama.

Controversies

The WBA has been plagued with charges of corruption for years. In perhaps the most notable instance, promoter Bob Arum claimed in a 1982 interview that he had to pay off WBA officials to obtain rankings. In a 1981 *Sports Illustrated* article, a WBA judge claimed that he was influenced by the WBA president to support certain fighters. The same article also discussed a variety of bribes paid to WBA officials to obtain title fights or rankings with the organization.

The WBA also came under fire in the 1980s for allowing South Africans to fight for its titles.[citation needed]

Regular titles and super titles

The WBA recognizes the title holders from the WBC, WBO and IBF organizations. The WBA refers to a champion who holds two or more of these titles in the same weight class as an "undisputed champion" or "super champion". This applies even if the WBA title is not one of the titles held by the "undisputed champion". In September 2008, Nate Campbell was recognized as lightweight "undisputed champion" for his WBO and IBF titles, while the WBA's own champion was Yusuke Kobori.

If one of the multiple titles held to earn the designation WBA Super Champion is the WBA's own title, then the fighter is promoted to Super Champion and their *regular* title becomes vacant for other WBA-ranked boxers to fight for. Thus, the WBA tables will sometimes show a WBA Super Champion and a WBA Regular Champion for the same weight class.

Sometimes it is possible for a regular champion to become super champion without adding another organization's title; Chris John is an example.

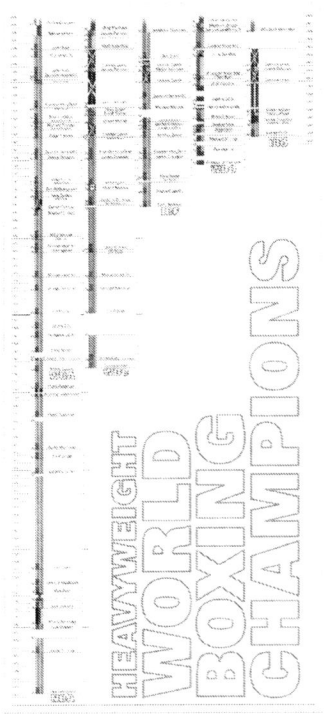

Champions since 1920 of heavyweight boxing of 5 most important Associations

Current WBA world title holders

Weight class:	Champion:	Date won:
Minimumweight	Vacant	
Light flyweight	Giovanni Segura	June 5, 2009
Flyweight	Daiki Kameda	February 7, 2010
Super flyweight	Vic Darchinyan (unified champion)	November 1, 2008
	Hugo Fidel Cazares (regular champion)	May 8, 2010
Bantamweight	Anselmo Moreno	May 31, 2008
Super bantamweight	Celestino Caballero (unified champion)	November 21, 2008
	Ryol Li Lee (regular champion)	October 2, 2010
Featherweight	Chris John (Super Champion)	June 27, 2009
	Yuriorkis Gamboa (regular champion)	June 27, 2009
Super featherweight	Takashi Uchiyama	January 11, 2010
Lightweight	Juan Manuel Márquez (unified champion)	February 28, 2009
	Miguel Acosta (regular champion)	May 29, 2010
Super lightweight	Amir Khan	July 18, 2009
Welterweight	Vyacheslav Senchenko	April 10, 2009
Super welterweight	Miguel Cotto (Super Champion)	June 5, 2010
Middleweight	Felix Sturm (Super Champion)	April 28, 2007
Super middleweight	Andre Ward (Super Champion)	November 21, 2009
	Dimitri Sartison (regular champion)	November 21, 2009
Light heavyweight	Beibut Shumenov	January 29, 2010
Cruiserweight	Guillermo Jones	September 27, 2008
Heavyweight	David Haye	November 7, 2009

See also

Other world organizations

- International Boxing Association
- International Boxing Council
- International Boxing Federation
- International Boxing Organization
- International Boxing Union
- World Boxing Council
- World Professional Boxing Federation & United States Boxing Council
- World Boxing Federation
- World Boxing Organization
- World Boxing Union

Regional Organizations

- North American Boxing Council
- List of Commonwealth Boxing Council Champions

WBA affiliated organizations

- FEDELATIN
- Pan Asian Boxing Association (PABA)
- European Boxing Association (EBA)
- North American Boxing Association (NABA)

Transition of WBA titles

- List of WBA world champions
- List of WBA international champions
- List of WBA Fedecentro champions
- List of WBA Fedelatin champions
- List of WBA Pan African champions
- List of WBA female world champions

External links

- WBA official homepage [1]
- All-time WBA World champions - Reference book [2]

Heavyweight

Heavyweight is a division, or weight class, in boxing. Fighters who weigh over 200 pounds (14 st 4 lb/91 kg) are considered heavyweights by the major professional boxing organizations: the International Boxing Organization, the World Boxing Association, the World Boxing Council, and the World Boxing Organization.

Because this division has no weight limit, it has been historically vaguely defined. In the 19th century, for example, many heavyweight champions weighed 170 pounds (12 st 2 lb, 77 kg) or less (although others weighed 200 pounds and more). In 1920, the minimum weight for a heavyweight was set at 175 pounds (12 st 7 lb, 79 kg), which today is the light heavyweight division maximum. Today, for most boxing organizations, the maximum weight for a cruiserweight is 200 pounds. Thus, a fighter whose weight is over 200 lb may not fight as anything but a heavyweight.

It is impossible to say with absolute certainty who the first heavyweight champion was, since the sport of boxing goes back as far as recorded history and there have always been large fighters. However, James Figg, "the father of modern pugilism", is most often referred to as the first champion of organized boxing. Even in the bare-knuckle era, "champions" were plentiful. Some of the most notable of these included the slave Tom Molineaux, Tom Cribb, Jack Slack, Jem Belcher, Ben Caunt and Jem Mace. The first heavyweight champion under the Marquess of Queensberry rules was John L. Sullivan, known as "The Boston Strong Boy." He weighed around 200 pounds when in shape and was a bare-knuckle champion. He was defeated by Jim Corbett on September 7, 1892, in 21 rounds.

It should also be noted that in recent years, the heavyweight title has become fractured amongst various sanctioning organizations, and so what was once known as the single "Heavyweight Champion," is now referred to as the "Undisputed Champion" as the one fighter that has defeated all the other titlists.

Professional champions

Current champions

Sanctioning Body	Reign Began	Champion	Record	Defenses
WBA	November 7, 2009	David Haye	24-1 (22 KO)	1
WBC	October 11, 2008	Vitali Klitschko	40-2 (38 KO)	4
IBF	April 22, 2006	Wladimir Klitschko	55-3 (49 KO)	9
WBO	February 23, 2008	Wladimir Klitschko	55-3 (49 KO)	5

- List of heavyweight boxing champions

Light heavyweight

In boxing, the **light heavyweight** (above 168 pounds [12 Stone or 76.204 kilograms] up to 175 pounds [12.5 stone or 79.38 kilograms]) division is the weight division between cruiserweight and super middleweight. The light heavyweight class has produced some of boxing's greatest champions: Muhammad Ali, Evander Holyfield, Tommy Loughran, Billy Conn, Joey Maxim, Archie Moore, Bob Foster, Michael Spinks, Roy Jones Jr, Joe Calzaghe and Bernard Hopkins to name a few.

Many light heavyweight champions unsuccessfully challenged for the heavyweight crown until Michael Spinks became the first reigning light heavyweight champion to win the heavyweight championship. Bob Fitzsimmons captured the light heavyweight championship after losing his heavyweight championship. Two all-time great heavyweight champions, Ezzard Charles and Floyd Patterson, started out as light heavyweights. Charles defeated Archie Moore and Joey Maxim several times in non-title bouts before becoming heavyweight champion and Patterson lost an eight-round decision to Joey Maxim before becoming heavyweight champion himself. Evander Holyfield successfully moved up from the light-heavyweight division to both the cruiser and eventually heavyweight divisions and became undisputed champion of both.

Olympic champions

- 1920 – Eddie Eagan (USA)
- 1924 – Harry Mitchell (GBR)
- 1928 – Víctor Avendaño (ARG)
- 1932 – David Carstens (RSA)
- 1936 – Roger Michelot (FRA)
- 1948 – George Hunter (RSA)
- 1952 – Norvel Lee (USA)
- 1956 – James Boyd (USA)
- 1960 – Cassius Clay (later Muhammad Ali) (USA)
- 1964 – Cosimo Pinto (ITA)
- 1968 – Danas Pozniakas (URS)
- 1972 – Mate Parlov (YUG)
- 1976 – Leon Spinks (USA)
- 1980 – Slobodan Kacar (YUG)
- 1984 – Anton Josipović (YUG)
- 1988 – Andrew Maynard (USA)
- 1992 – Torsten May (GER)
- 1996 – Vassiliy Jirov (KAZ)
- 2000 – Aleksandr Lebziak (RUS)
- 2004 – Andre Ward (USA)
- 2008 – Zhang Xiaoping (CHN)

Professional champions

Current champions

Sanctioning Body	Reign Began	Champion	Record	Defenses
WBA	January 29, 2010	Beibut Shumenov	10-1 (6 KO)	1
WBC	June 19, 2009	Jean Pascal	26-1 (16 KO)	3
IBF	August 28, 2009	Tavoris Cloud	21-0 (18 KO)	1
WBO	November 13, 2009	Juergen Braehmer	36-2 (29 KO)	2

- List of light heavyweight boxing champions

See also

- Boxing

List of heavyweight boxing champions

This is a chronological **list of world heavyweight boxing champions** since the introduction of the Marquess of Queensberry rules: Bare knuckle champions who fought under London Prize Ring rules are not listed here, as they were predominantly British.

Championship recognition

1885–1910

Champions were recognized by public acclamation. A champion in that era was a fighter who had a notable win over another fighter and kept winning afterward. Retirements or disputed results could lead to a championship being split among several men for periods of time. With only minor exceptions, the heavyweight division remained free from dual title-holders until the 1960s.

1910–1961

Heavyweight World Boxing
Champions since 1920-2008

Championship awarding organizations

- The International Boxing Union (IBU), formed in Paris in 1910. Changed name to European Boxing Union in 1946. It organised world title fights from 1913 to 1963 after which it was incorporated into the World Boxing Council (WBC).
- The New York State Athletic Commission (NYSAC), formed in 1920. It organised world title bouts until the early 1970s when it became a member of World Boxing Council (WBC).
- The National Boxing Association (NBA) formed in the USA in 1921.
- Other bodies including the National Sporting Club in Great Britain and the California State Athletic Commission awarded world titles but this did not affect the heavyweight division.

1961–present

Championship awarding organizations

- The World Boxing Association (WBA), founded in 1921 as the National Boxing Association (NBA); it changed its name in 1961 and allowed membership from outside the USA.
- The World Boxing Council (WBC), founded in 1963.
- The International Boxing Federation (IBF), founded in 1983.
- The World Boxing Organization (WBO), founded in 1988.

Reign began...	Reign ended	Champion	Recognition	Nationality
August 29, 1885	September 7, 1892	John L. Sullivan	Universal	American
Sullivan defeated Paddy Ryan in 1882 for the bare knuckle championship of America. With the lack of legimate challengers from outside America Sullivan gradually gained recognition as champion of the world. On August 29, 1885, he outpointed Dominic McCaffrey in Chester Park, Cincinnati, in a bout described as being "to decide the Marquess of Queensberry glove contest for the championship of the world"				
September 7, 1892	March 17, 1897	James J. Corbett	Universal	American
James J. Corbett announced his retirement from boxing in 1895 and nominated his protege Steve O'Donnell as his successor. Tradition demanded that O'Donnell win the world title in the ring so he was matched against the erratic Irish boxer Peter Maher. The bout took place at the Empire Athletic club, Maspeth, New York on 11 November 1895, Maher surprisingly defeated O'Donnell via first round knockout. The general public had little acceptance of the new champion and even Maher himself expressed a wish to fight Corbett for the "real" title. Maher defended his "world title" against the British-born Bob Fitzsimmons in Coahuila de Zaragoza, Mexico on February 21, 1896, and was himself the victim of a first round knockout. Fitzsimmons then fought another Irish fighter, Tom Sharkey of Dundalk on December 2, 1896, in San Francisco, the bout being billed for the heavyweight title. Sharkey was awarded victory by disqualification in round 8 by the referee, Wyatt Earp. Corbett announced his return to the ring late in 1896 and the claims of Maher, Fitzsimmons (until 1897) and Sharkey to be champion are usually ignored.				
March 17, 1897	June 9, 1899	Bob Fitzsimmons	Universal	British / American
Fitzsimmons became an American citizen in 1898.				
June 9, 1899	May 13, 1905[1]	James J. Jeffries	Universal	American
Jeffries was the first modern champion to relinquish the title, announcing his retirement and declaring that the winner of a match between Marvin Hart and Jack Root would be the next legitimate champion. Jeffries would return to the ring to face Jack Johnson.				
July 3, 1905	February 23, 1906	Marvin Hart	Universal	American
February 23, 1906	December 26, 1908	Tommy Burns	Universal	Canadian
December 26, 1908	April 5, 1915	Jack Johnson	Universal	American
Jack Johnson's refusal to honor an agreement made by his manager to defend against the British champion led the National Sporting Club in London, the most powerful body in boxing outside the USA, to withdraw recognition of Johnson as champion. They matched Canadian Sam Langford and the British champion William "Iron" Hague for their version of the title. Langford beat Hague on a fourth round knockout in London on May 24, 1909. Langford returned home to America and never pressed his claim to the title.				
April 5, 1915	July 4, 1919	Jess Willard	Universal	American

July 4, 1919	September 23, 1926	Jack Dempsey	Universal	American
September 23, 1926	July 31, 1928[2]	Gene Tunney	Universal	American

Tunney announced his retirement from professional boxing on July 31, 1928, relinquishing the championship.

June 12, 1930	January 7, 1931	Max Schmeling	Universal	German

Schmeling defeated Jack Sharkey to earn universal recognition as champion but was stripped of the NYSAC version of the title in 1931 for refusing a rematch with Sharkey. The NYSAC title reamined vacant until the two men eventually did fight in 1932.

January 7, 1931	June 21, 1932	Max Schmeling	NBA & IBU	German
June 21, 1932	June 29, 1933	Jack Sharkey	Universal	American
June 29, 1933	June 14, 1934	Primo Carnera	Universal	Italian
June 14, 1934	June 13, 1935	Max Baer	Universal	American

In late 1934 the International Boxing Union ordered world champion Max Baer to defend his title against the reigning European champion, Pierre Charles of Belgium. When Baer instead opted to fight James J. Braddock they withdrew recognition of him as champion. The IBU matched Charles with the American heavyweight George Godfrey for their version of the title with the fight taking place in Brussels, Belgium on 2 October 1935. Godfrey won a fifteen round points decision but did not press any claim to the championship and was inactive for the next two years. The IBU then recognized Baer's successor, James J. Braddock, as champion.

June 13, 1935	June 22, 1937	James J. Braddock	Universal	American
June 22, 1937	March 1, 1949[2]	Joe Louis	Universal	American

As of 2009, Louis still holds the record for holding the title longer than any man (11 years, 8 months and 8 days.)

June 22, 1949	September 27, 1950	Ezzard Charles	NBA	American

Charles won the vacant National Boxing Association championship in June 1949, but was not universally recognized as champion until June 1951.

June 6, 1950	June 16, 1951	Lee Savold	EBU	American

On the retirement of Joe Louis in March 1949, the European Boxing Union announced that a fight in May 1949 between Lee Savold of the USA and British champion Bruce Woodcock would determine their version of the world heavyweight title. The NYSAC and the British Boxing Board of Control (BBBofC) also decided to recognize the winner of the fight as their champion but it was postponed for over a year due to injuries Woodcock had suffered in a car crash. The NYSAC decided instead to recognize the winner of the upcoming bout in September 1950 between Ezzard Charles and Joe Louis as their champion. Louis was returning to the ring after an absence of 27 months. When the fight for the EBU and BBBofC world heavyweight titles eventually took place in June 1950, Savold defeated Woodcock in four rounds.

September 27, 1950	June 16, 1951	Ezzard Charles	NBA & NYSAC	American
June 16, 1951	July 18, 1951	Ezzard Charles	Universal	American

Following his defeat to Joe Louis in a non-title fight in June 1951, Lee Savold was no longer recognized as the world heavyweight champion by the EBU and the BBBofC, who both immediately transferred their recognition to Ezzard Charles. Charles therefore became universally recognized as world heavyweight champion.

July 18, 1951	September 23, 1952	Jersey Joe Walcott	Universal	American

September 23, 1952	November 30, 1956[2]	Rocky Marciano	Universal	American
Marciano announced his retirement from professional boxing, relinquishing the championship.				
November 30, 1956	June 26, 1959	Floyd Patterson	Universal	American
June 26, 1959	June 20, 1960	Ingemar Johansson	Universal	Swedish
June 20, 1960	September 25, 1962	Floyd Patterson	Universal	American
September 25, 1962	February 25, 1964	Sonny Liston	Universal	American
February 25, 1964	June 19, 1964	Cassius Clay (Muhammad Ali)	Universal	American
The WBA and the NYSAC withdrew their recognition of Clay (now known as Muhammad Ali) as champion for agreeing to an immediate rematch against Liston, a violation of the organization's rules at the time. The WBC and other organizations continued to recognize him. (See Ali versus Liston.)				
June 19, 1964	February 6, 1967	Cassius Clay (Muhammad Ali)	WBC	American
March 5, 1965	February 6, 1967	Ernie Terrell	WBA & NYSAC	American
February 6, 1967	April 29, 1967	Muhammad Ali	Universal	American
The WBA, the NYSAC and several other US state boxing commissions withdrew recognition of Ali as champion for his refusal to be inducted into the United States Army subsequent to being drafted in early 1967.				
April 29, 1967	March, 1969	Muhammad Ali	WBC	American
The WBC eventually followed the lead of the WBA and the NYSAC and stripped Ali of their title in March 1969.				
March 4, 1968	February 16, 1970	Joe Frazier	NYSAC	American
April 28, 1968	February 16, 1970	Jimmy Ellis	WBA	American
February 16, 1970	January 22, 1973	Joe Frazier	Universal	American
Frazier and Ellis fought on February 16, 1970, at Madison Square Garden, New York. Frazier entered the ring as the holder of NYSAC version of the world title and Ellis held the WBA heavyweight title. The fight was also for the WBC title vacated by Muhammad Ali. Frazier defeated Ellis and was universally recognized as champion. He cemented his reputation upon defeating Muhammad Ali on March 8, 1971. (See Fight of the Century)				
January 22, 1973	October 30, 1974	George Foreman	Universal	American
October 30, 1974	February 15, 1978	Muhammad Ali	Universal	American
February 15, 1978	March 18, 1978[3]	Leon Spinks	Universal	American
March 18, 1978	September 15, 1978	Leon Spinks	WBA	American
March 18, 1978	June 9, 1978	Ken Norton	WBC	American
Spinks was stripped of his world title by the WBC for refusing to defend his title against their #1 ranked contender, Ken Norton. Spinks instead agreed to fight a return bout against Ali for the WBA crown. The WBC awarded Norton the title and, since he lost to Larry Holmes in his next defense, he is sometimes omitted from a list of heavyweight champions because he never won a world title fight.				

June 9, 1978	December 11, 1983[1]	Larry Holmes	WBC	American
Holmes relinquished his WBC title to assume the championship of the newly formed International Boxing Federation.				
September 15, 1978	April 27, 1979[1]	Muhammad Ali	WBA	American
Believing his career over, Ali relinquished his WBA title in exchange for a payment from promoter Don King, who was trying to stage a bout between then-WBC champ Larry Holmes and John Tate for the undisputed title. The bout never materialized, and Ali would return to the ring in 1980.				
October 20, 1979	March 31, 1980	John Tate	WBA	American
March 31, 1980	December 10, 1982	Mike Weaver	WBA	American
December 10, 1982	September 23, 1983	Michael Dokes	WBA	American
September 23, 1983	December 1, 1984	Gerrie Coetzee	WBA	South African
December 11, 1983	September 21, 1985	Larry Holmes	IBF	American
March 9, 1984	August 31, 1984	Tim Witherspoon	WBC	American
August 31, 1984	March 22, 1986	Pinklon Thomas	WBC	American
December 1, 1984	April 29, 1985	Greg Page	WBA	American
April 29, 1985	January 17, 1986	Tony Tubbs	WBA	American
September 21, 1985	February 19, 1987[3]	Michael Spinks	IBF	American
January 17, 1986	December 12, 1986	Tim Witherspoon	WBA	American
March 22, 1986	November 22, 1986	Trevor Berbick	WBC	Canadian / Jamaican
Jamaican born Berbick was a naturalized Canadian citizen and former Canadian heavyweight champion.				
November 22, 1986	March 7, 1987	Mike Tyson	WBC	American
December 12, 1986	March 7, 1987	James 'Bonecrusher' Smith	WBA	American
March 7, 1987	August 1, 1987	Mike Tyson	WBA & WBC	American
May 30, 1987	August 1, 1987	Tony Tucker	IBF	American
August 1, 1987	May 6, 1989	Mike Tyson	Universal	American
May 6, 1989	January 11, 1991	Francesco Damiani	WBO	Italian
Though Damiani defeated Johnny DuPlooy to become the WBO's first Heavyweight champion, Tyson's reign in the division during this period is virtually undisputed. Additionally, during this period Tyson also knocked out Michael Spinks who some regarded as the 'lineal champion.'				
May 6, 1989	February 11, 1990	Mike Tyson	IBF, WBA & WBC	American
February 11, 1990	October 25, 1990	James "Buster" Douglas	IBF, WBA & WBC	American
October 25, 1990	November 13, 1992	Evander Holyfield	IBF, WBA & WBC	American

January 11, 1991	December 24, 1991[3]	Ray Mercer	WBO	American
May 15, 1992	February 3, 1993[3]	Michael Moorer	WBO	American
November 13, 1992	December 14, 1992[3]	Riddick Bowe	IBF, WBA & WBC	American

Bowe was stripped of his WBC championship for refusing to fight Lennox Lewis.

December 14, 1992	November 6, 1993	Riddick Bowe	IBF & WBA	American
December 14, 1992	September 24, 1994	Lennox Lewis	WBC	British

Lewis was born in England but moved to Ontario, Canada at the age of 12, later winning an Olympic gold medal for Canada. Lewis defeated Razor Ruddock on October 31, 1992, in a WBC 'eliminator' fight. When Riddick Bowe's championship recognition was withdrawn by the organization, the WBC immediately awarded Lewis the title.

June 7, 1993	October 29, 1993	Tommy Morrison	WBO	American
October 29, 1993	March 19, 1994	Michael Bentt	WBO	American
November 6, 1993	April 22, 1994	Evander Holyfield	IBF & WBA	American
March 19, 1994	March 11, 1995	Herbie Hide	WBO	British
April 22, 1994	November 5, 1994	Michael Moorer	IBF & WBA	American
September 24, 1994	September 2, 1995	Oliver McCall	WBC	American
November 5, 1994	March 4, 1995[3]	George Foreman	IBF & WBA	American

The World Boxing Association withdrew its recognition of Foreman, but Foreman retained IBF championship recognition until it too was withdrawn.

March 4, 1995	June 28, 1995[3]	George Foreman	IBF	American

The IBF withdrew its recognition of Foreman when he declined a rematch with Axel Schulz of Germany. Schultz was matched with Francois Botha of South Africa for the vacant title. The bout took place on December 9, 1995 in Stuttgart and resulted in a split decision points victory for Botha. Botha however tested positive for illegal anabolic steroids in a post-fight drugs test and the result was changed to a no-contest. Although some record books continue to list Botha as a world champion, the IBF state that they do not regard that he was ever champion.

March 11, 1995	May 1, 1996[1]	Riddick Bowe	WBO	American
April 8, 1995	September 7, 1996	Bruce Seldon	WBA	American
September 2, 1995	March 16, 1996	Frank Bruno	WBC	British
March 16, 1996	September 7, 1996	Mike Tyson	WBC	American
June 22, 1996	November 8, 1997	Michael Moorer	IBF	American
June 29, 1996	February 17, 1997[1]	Henry Akinwande	WBO	British

Akinwande had been ranked the WBC's #2 contender when he won the WBO title. The WBC, which has feuded with the WBO since the latter's founding in 1988, dropped Akinwande from its rankings altogether. Akinwande subsequently relinquished his WBO title in exchange for the opportunity to meet Lennox Lewis in a bout for the WBC championship.

September 7, 1996	September 24, 1996[1]	Mike Tyson	WBA & WBC	American
September 24, 1996	November 9, 1996	Mike Tyson	WBA	American
November 9, 1996	November 8, 1997	Evander Holyfield	WBA	American
February 7, 1997	November 13, 1999	Lennox Lewis	WBC	British
June 28, 1997	June 26, 1999	Herbie Hide	WBO	British
November 8, 1997	November 13, 1999	Evander Holyfield	IBF & WBA	American
June 26, 1999	April 1, 2000	Vitali Klitschko	WBO	Ukrainian
November 13, 1999	April 29, 2000[3]	Lennox Lewis	IBF, WBA & WBC	British

In early 2000 the World Boxing Association and Lewis were sued by representatives of John Ruiz claiming that they had reneged on an agreement by which Ruiz would have fought Lewis for the WBA title. A New Jersey court ruled in favor of Ruiz, and ordered Lewis to either have his next bout against Ruiz or relinquish the title. Lewis elected instead to fight contender Michael Grant, relinquishing his WBA title on the day of the match.

April 1, 2000	October 14, 2000	Chris Byrd	WBO	American
April 29, 2000	April 22, 2001	Lennox Lewis	IBF & WBC	British
August 12, 2000	March 3, 2001	Evander Holyfield	WBA	American
October 14, 2000	March 8, 2003	Wladimir Klitschko	WBO	Ukrainian
March 3, 2001	March 1, 2003	John Ruiz	WBA	American
April 22, 2001	November 17, 2001	Hasim Rahman	IBF & WBC	American
November 17, 2001	September 5, 2002[1]	Lennox Lewis	IBF & WBC	British

Lewis relinquished the IBF title upon receiving payment of $1 million (US) by promoter Don King, who wished to stage a bout between Chris Byrd and Evander Holyfield for the vacant title.

September 5, 2002	February 6, 2004[2]	Lennox Lewis	WBC	British
December 14, 2002	April 22, 2006	Chris Byrd	IBF	American
March 1, 2003	February 20, 2004[1]	Roy Jones Jr.	WBA	American
March 8, 2003	October 9, 2003[1]	Corrie Sanders	WBO	South African
February 20, 2004	December 17, 2005	John Ruiz	WBA	American

Ruiz beat Hasim Rahman on December 13, 2003, to become the WBA's "interim" champion. He was awarded the championship following Roy Jones, Jr.'s announcement that he was relinquishing it to concentrate on lower weight divisions. Ruiz's title reign ended on April 30, 2005, following a loss to James Toney but ten days later, a drug test on Toney detected he had used products containing nandrolone, an anabolic steroid. Thus, Toney's victory was changed to a 'no contest' by New York state athletic commission, and as a result, the WBA declared Ruiz was keeping the title.

April 10, 2004	April 1, 2006	Lamon Brewster	WBO	American

April 24, 2004	November 9, 2005[2]	Vitali Klitschko	WBC	Ukrainian
November 9, 2005	August 13, 2006	Hasim Rahman	WBC	American

Rahman defeated Monte Barrett on August 13, 2005, to become the WBC's "interim" champion. He was awarded the championship following Vitali Klitschko's announcement that he was retiring due to injury.

December 17, 2005	April 15, 2007	Nikolay Valuev	WBA	Russian
April 1, 2006	November 4, 2006	Sergei Liakhovich	WBO	Belarusian
April 22, 2006	February 23, 2008	Wladimir Klitschko	IBF	Ukrainian
August 13, 2006	March 8, 2008	Oleg Maskaev	WBC	American/Russian

Maskaev was born in Kazakhstan to Russian parents. He originally held Kazakh citizenship but was granted US citizenship in 2004. In December 2006 he was also granted Russian citizenship. On September 24, 2007, Samuel Peter was declared the WBC's "interim" champion. Peter ultimately defeated Maskaev on March 8, 2008.

November 4, 2006	June 2, 2007	Shannon Briggs	WBO	American
April 15, 2007	July 4, 2008[4]	Ruslan Chagaev	WBA	Uzbekistani

Chagaev's mandatory title defence against former champion Nikolay Valuev, scheduled for July 5, 2008, had to be cancelled for a second time after Chagaev suffered a complete tear of an Achilles tendon during his training for the fight. Because of the injury and necessary recovery time, the WBA elected to make Chagaev "Champion In Recess" and mandated that top-contenders Valuev and John Ruiz meet for the title. They set a deadline of June 26, 2009 for Chagaev to fight the champion but as this deadline was not met, Chagaev was stripped of his "Champion In Recess" title when the WBA published their Official Ratings as of June 2009.

June 2, 2007	February 23, 2008	Sultan Ibragimov	WBO	Russian
February 23, 2008	present	Wladimir Klitschko	IBF, WBO & IBO	Ukrainian
March 8, 2008	October 11, 2008	Samuel Peter	WBC	Nigerian
July 4, 2008[4]	July 24, 2009	Ruslan Chagaev	WBA	Uzbekistani

The WBA had set a deadline of June 26, 2009 for Chagaev to fight the champion but this deadline was not met. On July 24, 2009, when the WBA published their Official Ratings as of June 2009, Chagaev was stripped of his "Champion In Recess" title.

August 30, 2008	November 7, 2009	Nikolay Valuev	WBA	Russian

Valuev regained the WBA title by beating John Ruiz on August 30, 2008, shortly after Chagaev had become the "Champion In Recess". Upon making Chagaev the "Champion In Recess", the WBA set a deadline of June 26, 2009 for him to fight the champion. This deadline was not met and Chagaev was stripped of his "Champion In Recess" title when the WBA published their Official Ratings as of June 2009.

October 11, 2008	November 7 2009	Vitali Klitschko	WBC	Ukrainian
November 7, 2009	present	David Haye	WBA	British

In 2010 Haye was awarded citizenship of North Cyprus. A state whose existence is recognized only by Turkey.

Footnotes

1. Relinquished championship title.
2. Retired as champion, relinquishing title.
3. Championship recognition withdrawn by sanctioning organization due to champion's failure or refusal to defend title against the organization's #1 ranked contender.
4. Status as champion changed from "Champion" to "Champion In Recess".

Sources

- Arnold, Peter (1989). *Encyclopedia of Boxing*. London: WH Smith Books. ISBN 1-85435-200-8.
- World Title Lineages [1]

See also

- List of current world boxing champions

Personal life

Lawrenceville, Georgia

Lawrenceville, Georgia
— City —

Gwinnett County Courthouse
Nickname(s): The Crepe Myrtle City, L'ville, Lowdown
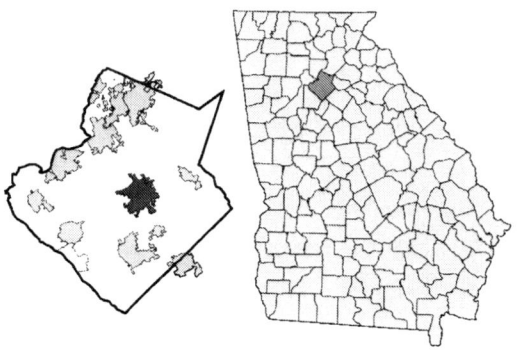
Location in Gwinnett County and the state of Georgia
Coordinates: 33°57′11″N 83°59′33″W

Country	United States
State	Georgia
County	Gwinnett

Area	
- Total	13.1 sq mi (33.7 km^2)
- Land	13 sq mi (33.6 km^2)
- Water	0.1 sq mi (0.1 km^2)
Elevation	1066 ft (325 m)
Population (2000)	
- Total	29837
- Density	1709.7/sq mi (664.6/km^2)
Time zone	Eastern (EST) (UTC-5)
- Summer (DST)	EDT (UTC-4)
ZIP codes	30042-30046, 30049
Area code(s)	404/678/770
FIPS code	13-45488
GNIS feature ID	0316699

Lawrenceville is a city in and the county seat of Gwinnett County, Georgia, in the United States. The 2000 census recorded the city's population as 22,397. The Census Bureau estimates the 2008 population at 29,258. Lawrenceville has six ZIP codes (30042-30046, 30049); it is part of the 678/770/404 telephone area code, which is used throughout metropolitan Atlanta.

History

Lawrenceville was incorporated by an act of the Georgia General Assembly on 15 December 1821. This makes Lawrenceville one of the oldest cities in the Metro Atlanta Area. The city is named after Commodore James Lawrence, commander of the Frigate Chesapeake during the War of 1812. In 1821 a permanent site for the county courthouse was selected and purchased, the four streets bordering the square were laid out along with other streets in the village, and a public well was dug. Major Grace built the first permanent courthouse, a brick structure, in 1823-24 for a cost of $4,000. The courthouse presently on the square was constructed in 1885.

William Maltbie, the town's first postmaster, suggested the name "Lawrenceville" in honor of Captain James Lawrence, a naval commander during the War of 1812. Lawrence, a native of New Jersey, is probably best known today for his dying command, "Don't give up the ship!"

Courtland Winn served two terms as mayor starting in 1884 when he was 21 years old.

The two most famous people born in Lawrenceville gained their fame elsewhere. Charles Henry Smith, born in 1826, left as a young man and lived most of his life in other Georgia towns. Beginning during the Civil War, he wrote humorous pieces for Atlanta newspapers under the name Bill Arp. He has been described as the South's most popular writer of the late 19th century, though he is not much read today. Ezzard Charles, born in Lawrenceville in 1921, grew up in Cincinnati, where opportunities for African-Americans were far better at the time than in the Deep South. He eventually was heavyweight boxing champion of the world.

As a boy, Oliver Hardy lived in downtown Lawrenceville around 1900. But the future movie star's stay was brief. His family moved often within Georgia.

Lawrenceville was one of many venues in the nation where *Hustler* magazine publisher Larry Flynt faced obscenity charges in the late 1970s. On March 6, 1978, during a lunch break in his Lawrenceville trial, he and his local attorney Gene Reeves were shot by a sniper near the courthouse. Both survived, though Flynt was seriously disabled. Imprisoned serial killer Joseph Paul Franklin claims to have been the shooter, but he did not make the claim until years after the crime, and he has never been charged in the case. A heavily fictionalized treatment of the shooting can be seen in the 1996 movie *The People vs. Larry Flynt*.

Geography

Lawrenceville is located at 33°57′11″N 83°59′33″W (33.953052, -83.992469). According to the United States Census Bureau, the city has a total area of 13.1 square miles (33.8 km²), of which, 13.0 square miles (33.6 km²) of it is land and 0.1 square miles (0.2 km²) of it (0.46%) is water.

Dacula, Duluth, Buford, Grayson, Lilburn, Norcross, Snellville, and Suwanee are nearby cities.

Climate

Lawrenceville has a humid subtropical climate (Köppen climate classification *Cfa*).

Climate data for Lawrenceville													
Month	Jan	Feb	Mar	Apr	May	Jun	Jul	Aug	Sep	Oct	Nov	Dec	Year
Average high °F (°C)	50 (10)	55 (12.8)	63 (17.2)	72 (22.2)	79 (26.1)	85 (29.4)	88 (31.1)	87 (30.6)	81 (27.2)	71 (21.7)	62 (16.7)	53 (11.7)	71 (21.7)
Average low °F (°C)	31 (-0.6)	32 (0)	39 (3.9)	45 (7.2)	54 (12.2)	63 (17.2)	67 (19.4)	66 (18.9)	60 (15.6)	49 (9.4)	40 (4.4)	33 (0.6)	48 (8.9)
Precipitation inches (mm)	5.32 (135.1)	4.39 (111.5)	5.48 (139.2)	3.87 (98.3)	3.94 (100.1)	3.78 (96)	4.02 (102.1)	3.71 (94.2)	3.98 (101.1)	3.74 (95)	3.63 (92.2)	3.77 (95.8)	49.63 (1260.6)

Source:

Demographics

Historical populations		
Census	Pop.	%±
1960	3804	—
1970	5115	34.5%
1980	8928	74.5%
1990	17250	93.2%
2000	22397	29.8%

As of the census of 2009, there were 29,397 people, 7,484 households, and 5,313 families residing in the city. The population density was 1,723.9 people per square mile (665.7/km²). There were 7,684 housing units at an average density of 591.5/sq mi (228.4/km²). The racial makeup of the city was 48.04% White, 40.61% African American, 0.22% Native American, 1.17% Asian, 0.10% Pacific Islander, 1.46% from other races, and 2.41% from two or more races. Hispanic or Latino of any race were 15.14% of the population.

In 2000, there were 7,484 households out of which 39.4% had children under the age of 18 living with them, 52.7% were married couples living together, 13.3% had a female householder with no husband present, and 29.0% were non-families. 23.0% of all households were made up of individuals and 8.5% had someone living alone who was 65 years of age or older. Self-reported same-sex unmarried-partner households account for 0.6% of all households. The average household size was 2.77 and the average family size was 3.24.

In the city the population was spread out with 26.4% under the age of 18, 11.0% from 18 to 24, 35.3% from 25 to 44, 18.2% from 45 to 64, and 9.1% who were 65 years of age or older. The median age was 32 years. For every 100 females there were 105.1 males. For every 100 females age 18 and over, there were 103.9 males.

The median income for a household in the city was $43,299, and the median income for a family was $48,557. Males had a median income of $34,263 versus $26,903 for females. The per capita income for the city was $19,649. About 11.7% of families and 24.5% of the population were below the poverty line, including 16.0% of those under age 18 and 11.9% of those age 65 or over.

Lawrenceville is the most populous incorporated city in Gwinnett County.

Transportation

Lawrenceville can be accessed through several highways. Georgia 316 passes through Lawrenceville to Athens and connects to Interstate 85 at Exit 106. Interstate 85 South then travels through downtown Atlanta, which is roughly 30 to 35 miles away. Lawrenceville can also be accessed by US 78 (Stone Mountain Freeway) and then Scenic Highway (Georgia 124) via Snellville, GA. Thirdly, some southern unincorporated areas with Lawrenceville addresses can be accessed by Ronald Reagan Parkway. Other highways that pass through Lawrenceville are US 29, GA 8, GA 20, and GA 120.

Lawrenceville also is home to Gwinnett's only airport, the small Gwinnett County Airport-Briscoe Field, which is not an international airport but serves some commercial (though mainly private) aircraft.

Education

Gwinnett County Public Schools operates public schools.

Schools with Lawrenceville mailing address

The following is a list of schools with a Lawrenceville mailing address, with its high school cluster in parenthesis.

Elementary Schools

- Cedar Hill Elementary School (Central Gwinnett)
- Lawrenceville Elementary School (Central Gwinnett)
- Simonton Elementary School (Central Gwinnett)
- Margaret Winn Holt Elementary School (Central Gwinnett)
- Benefield Elementary (Berkmar)
- Woodward Mill Elementary School
- Lovin Elementary School

Middle Schools

- Central Gwinnett Cluster Middle School (Central Gwinnett) (opening in August 2011)
- J.E. Richards Middle School (Central Gwinnett)

High Schools

- Central Gwinnett High School
- Phoenix High School
- Mountain View High School
- Archer High School

Other Schools

- Gwinnett InterVention Education (GIVE) Center East (Alternative School)
- Hooper Renwick School

Colleges and university

Within Lawrenceville are two public colleges:

- Gwinnett Technical College
- Georgia Gwinnett College

Libraries

Gwinnett County Public Library operates the Lawrenceville Branch in an unincorporated area.

Hospitals

Lawrenceville is home to one of the premier hospitals in the region, Gwinnett Medical Center. GMC is a non-profit, 500-bed health care network based in Gwinnett County. It comprises two hospitals, plus several supporting medical facilities, with more than 4,300 employees and more than 800 affiliated physicians. The flagship campus of GMC is located in Lawrenceville near the intersection of Hwy. 316 and Duluth Highway 120.

Downtown

Historically significant buildings in downtown Lawrenceville include the Gwinnett Historic Courthouse and Lawrenceville Female Seminary. Also downtown are various landmarks and antique locations. The downtown area includes many restaurants like UpTown Café, Corner Stop Café, Cosmo's Original Little Italy Pizza, and McCray's Tavern on the Square. Downtown also offers valuable living on the square with the new "Cornerstone On The Square" condos and townhomes. Lawrenceville's revitalization plan was strengthened in 2005 when the city crafted a unique partnership with the Aurora Theatre [1] (Gwinnett county's only professional theatre), which relocated from the nearby town of Duluth to a permanent site in downtown Lawrenceville in May 2007 for the opening of its eleventh season. Another theater is GTC on Gwinnett Drive. The Aurora Theatre also conducts Lawrenceville Ghost Tours [2]--a 90 minute walking tour of the historic downtown area lead by professional storytellers. Ghost tour guides recount town lore and legends including Lawrenceville's role in the trial of Larry Flynt and the kidnapping of Barbara Jane Mackle.

Sports

The AAA minor league baseball Gwinnett Braves of the International League play at Coolray Field.

Notable natives and residents

- Robert Craig
- Ezzard Charles
- EJay Day
- Darius Walker
- Courtland Winn
- Brian McCann
- Jeff Francouer
- Jonathan Babineaux
- Jennifer Ferrin
- Hamilton Jordan
- Junior Samples
- Toby Sells (Special Make-up FX Artist)
- Rachel G. Fox (Actress from *Desperate Housewives)*

Trivia

- Deion Sanders once bought land in Lawrenceville to build a mansion, but sold it to construction companies.
- The film *Road Trip* was filmed in parts of Lawrenceville.

External links

- City of Lawrenceville [3]
- Georgia.gov: Lawrenceville [4]
- Web site of the Courts of Gwinnett County [5]
- Gwinnett County Public Schools [6]
- Gwinnett County Public Library [7]
- Lawrenceville Tourism & Trade Association [8]
- Listen to the Lawrenceville Police Department [9]

African American

African American

Frederick Douglass · Barack Obama · Rosa Parks
Condoleezza Rice · M. L. King, Jr. · Beyoncé Knowles
Malcolm X · Oprah Winfrey · Booker T. Washington
Michael Jordan · Harriet Tubman · Muhammad Ali

Total population

African American
37,586,050
(~12% of the US population)
Non-Hispanic Black
36,701,103
Black Hispanic
884,947

Regions with significant populations

Throughout the Southern United States, Northeastern United States, parts of the Midwestern United States, California

Languages

American English · African American Vernacular English · minorities speak Spanish · French · Brazilian Portuguese · Haitian Creole · African languages

Religion

Protestantism · Catholicism · Islam
Related ethnic groups
Americo-Liberian · Afro-Latin American · Black Hispanic and Latino Americans

African Americans (also referred to as **Black Americans** or **Afro-Americans**, and formerly as **American Negroes**) are citizens or residents of the United States who have origins in any of the black populations of Africa. In the United States, the terms are generally used for Americans with at least partial Sub-Saharan African ancestry.

Most African Americans are the direct descendants of captive Africans who survived the slavery era within the boundaries of the present United States, although some are—or are descended from—immigrants from African, Caribbean, Central American or South American nations. As an adjective, the term is usually spelled *African-American.*

African-American history starts in the 17th century with indentured servitude in the American colonies and progresses onto the election of an African American as the 44th and current President of the United States—Barack Obama. Between those landmarks there were other events and issues, both resolved and ongoing, that were faced by African Americans. Some of these were slavery, reconstruction, development of the African-American community, participation in the great military conflicts of the United States, racial segregation, and the Civil Rights Movement.

Black Americans make up the single largest racial minority in the United States and form the second largest racial group after whites in the United States.

History

Main article: African American history

Slavery era

An artist's conception of Crispus Attucks (1723–1770), the first "martyr" of the American Revolution.

Main articles: Slavery in the United States and Atlantic slave trade

The first recorded Africans in British North America (including most of the future United States) arrived in 1619 as indentured servants who settled in Jamestown, Virginia. As English settlers died from harsh conditions more and more Africans were brought to work as laborers. Africans for many years were similar in legal position to poor English indenturees, who traded several years labor in exchange for passage to America.

Africans could legally raise crops and cattle to purchase their freedom. They raised families, marrying other Africans and sometimes intermarrying with Native Americans or English settlers. By the 1640s and 1650s, several African families owned farms around Jamestown and some became wealthy by colonial standards.

The popular conception of a race-based slave system did not fully develop until the 18th century. The first black congregations and churches were organized before 1800 in both northern and southern cities following the Great Awakening. By 1775, Africans made up 20% of the population in the American colonies, which made them the second largest ethnic group after the English.

During the 1770s Africans, both enslaved and free, helped rebellious English colonists secure American Independence by defeating the British in the American Revolution. Africans and Englishmen fought side by side and were fully integrated. James Armistead, an African American, played a large part in making possible the 1781 Yorktown victory, which established the United States as an independent nation. Other prominent African Americans were Prince Whipple and Oliver Cromwell, who are both depicted in the front of the boat in George Washington's famous *1776 Crossing the Delaware* portrait.

By 1860, there were 3.5 million enslaved African Americans in the United States due to the Atlantic slave trade, and another 500,000 African Americans lived free across the country. In 1863, during the American Civil War, President Abraham Lincoln signed the Emancipation Proclamation. The proclamation declared that all slaves in states which had seceded from the Union were free. Advancing

Union troops enforced the proclamation with Texas being the last state to be emancipated in 1865.

Reconstruction and Jim Crow

Main articles: Reconstruction era of the United States and Jim Crow laws

African Americans quickly set up congregations for themselves, as well as schools, community and civic associations, to have space away from white control or oversight. While the post-war reconstruction era was initially a time of progress for African Americans, in the late 1890s, Southern states enacted Jim Crow laws to enforce racial segregation and disenfranchisement. Most African Americans followed the Jim Crow laws, using a mask of compliance to prevent becoming victims of racially motivated violence. To maintain self-esteem and dignity, African Americans such as Anthony Overton and Mary McLeod Bethune continued to build their own schools, churches, banks, social clubs, and other businesses.

Jesse Owens shook racial stereotypes both with Aryan Nazis and segregationists in the USA at the 1936 Berlin olympics.

In the last decade of the 19th century, racially discriminatory laws and racial violence aimed at African Americans began to mushroom in the United States. These discriminatory acts included racial segregation—upheld by the United States Supreme Court decision in Plessy v. Ferguson in 1896—which was legally mandated by southern states and nationwide at the local level of government, voter suppression or disenfranchisement in the southern states, denial of economic opportunity or resources nationwide, and private acts of violence and mass racial violence aimed at African Americans unhindered or encouraged by government authorities.

Great Migration and Civil Rights Movement

Main articles: Great Migration (African American) and African-American Civil Rights Movement (1955–1968)

The desperate conditions of African Americans in the South that sparked the Great Migration of the early 20th century, combined with a growing African American intellectual and cultural elite in the Northern United States, led to a movement to fight violence and discrimination against African Americans that, like abolitionism before it, crossed racial lines.

An African American boy outside of Cincinnati, Ohio in the 1940s

The Civil Rights Movement between 1954 to 1968 was directed at abolishing racial discrimination against African Americans, particularly in the Southern United States. The March on Washington for Jobs and Freedom and the conditions which brought it into being are credited with putting pressure on President John F. Kennedy and then Lyndon B. Johnson.

Johnson put his support behind passage of the Civil Rights Act of 1964 that banned discrimination in public accommodations, employment, and labor unions, and the Voting Rights Act (1965), which expanded federal authority over states to ensure black political participation through

March on Washington, August 28, 1963, shows civil rights and union leaders

protection of voter registration and elections. By 1966, the emergence of the Black Power movement, which lasted from 1966 to 1975, expanded upon the aims of the Civil Rights Movement to include economic and political self-sufficiency, and freedom from white authority.

Post Civil Rights Era African-American history

Main article: Post Civil Rights Era African-American history

Politically and economically, blacks have made substantial strides in the post-civil rights era. In 1989, Douglas Wilder became the first African-American elected governor in U.S. history. There are currently two black governors serving concurrently; governor Deval Patrick of Massachusetts and governor David Paterson of New York. Clarence Thomas became the second African-American Supreme Court Justice.In 1992 Carol Moseley-Braun of Illinois became the first black woman elected to the U.S. Senate. There were 8,936 black officeholders in the United States in 2000, showing a net increase of 7,467 since 1970. In 2001 there were 484 black mayors.

On November 4, 2008, Democratic then-Senator Barack Obama defeated Republican Senator John McCain to become the first black American to be elected President of the United States. At least 95 percent of African-American voters voted for Obama. He also received overwhelming support from young and educated whites, a majority of Asians, Americans of Hispanic origin, and Native AmericansWikipedia:Verifiability picking up a number of new states in the Democratic electoral column. Obama lost the overall white vote, although he won a larger proportion of white votes than any previous nonincumbent Democratic presidential candidate since Jimmy Carter. The following year Michael S. Steele was elected the first African-American chairman of the national Republican Party.

Demographics

Further information: List of U.S. communities with African American majority populations and List of U.S. counties with African American majority populations

In 1790, when the first U.S. Census was taken, Africans (including slaves and free people) numbered about 760,000—about 19.3% of the population. In 1860, at the start of the American Civil War, the African American population had increased to 4.4 million, but the percentage rate dropped to 14% of the overall population of the country. The vast majority were slaves, with only 488,000 counted as "freemen". By 1900, the black population had doubled and reached 8.8 million.

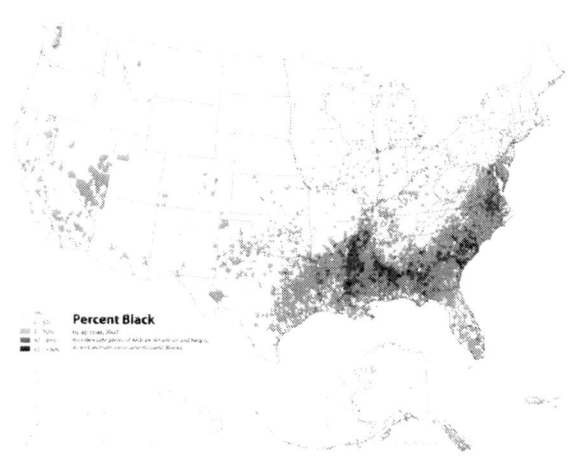

African Americans as percent of population, 2000.

In 1910, about 90% of African Americans lived in the South, but large numbers began migrating north looking for better job opportunities and living conditions, and to escape Jim Crow laws and racial violence. The Great Migration, as it was called, spanned the 1890s to the 1970s. From 1916 through the 1960s, more than 6 million black people moved north. But in the 1970s and 1980s, that trend reversed, with more African Americans moving south to the Sun Belt than leaving it.

The following table of the African American population in the United States over time shows that the African American population, as a percent of the total population, declined until 1930 and has been rising since then.

Year	Number	% of total population	Slaves	% in slavery
1790	757,208	19.3% (highest)	697,681	92%
1800	1,002,037	18.9%	893,602	89%
1810	1,377,808	19.0%	1,191,362	86%
1820	1,771,656	18.4%	1,538,022	87%
1830	2,328,642	18.1%	2,009,043	86%
1840	2,873,648	16.8%	2,487,355	87%
1850	3,638,808	15.7%	3,204,287	88%
1860	4,441,830	14.1%	3,953,731	89%
1870	4,880,009	12.7%	–	–
1880	6,580,793	13.1%	–	–
1890	7,488,788	11.9%	–	–
1900	8,833,994	11.6%	–	–
1910	9,827,763	10.7%	–	–
1920	10.5 million	9.9%	–	–
1930	11.9 million	9.7% (lowest)	–	–
1940	12.9 million	9.8%	–	–
1950	15.0 million	10.0%	–	–
1960	18.9 million	10.5%	–	–
1970	22.6 million	11.1%	–	–
1980	26.5 million	11.7%	–	–
1990	30.0 million	12.1%	–	–
2000	36.6 million	12.3%	–	–

By 1990, the African American population reached about 30 million and represented 12% of the U.S. population, roughly the same proportion as in 1900. In current demographics, according to 2005 U.S. CensusWikipedia:Disputed statement figures, some 39.9 million African Americans live in the United States, comprising 13.8% of the total population. The World Factbook gives a 2006 figure of 12.9% Controversy has surrounded the "accurate" population count of African Americans for decades. The NAACP believed it was under counted intentionally to minimize the significance of the black population in order to reduce their political power base.

At the time of the 2000 Census, 54.8% of African Americans lived in the South. In that year, 17.6% of African Americans lived in the Northeast and 18.7% in the Midwest, while only 8.9% lived in the western states. The west does have a sizable black population in certain areas, however. California, the nation's most populous state, has the fifth largest African American population, only behind New York, Texas, Georgia, and Florida. According to the 2000 Census, approximately 2.05% of African Americans identified as Hispanic or Latino in origin, many of whom may be of Brazilian, Puerto Rican, Dominican, Cuban, Haitian, or other Latin American descent.

The only self-reported ancestral groups larger than African Americans are Irish Americans and German Americans. Because many African Americans trace their ancestry to colonial American origins, some simply self-identify as "American".[citation needed]

U.S. cities

Further information: List of U.S. cities with large African American populations and List of U.S. metropolitan areas with large African-American populations

Almost 58% of African Americans lived in metropolitan areas in 2000. With over 2 million black residents, New York City had the largest black urban population in the United States in 2000, overall the city has a 28% black population. Chicago has the second largest black population, with almost 1.6 million African Americans in its metropolitan area, representing about 18 percent of the total metropolitan population.

Among cities of 100,000 or more, Gary, Indiana had the highest percentage of black residents of any U.S. city in 2000, with 84% (though it should be noted that the 2006 Census estimate puts the city's population below 100,000). Gary is followed closely by Detroit, Michigan, which was 82% African American. Other large cities with African American majorities include New Orleans, Louisiana (67%), Baltimore, Maryland (64%) Atlanta, Georgia (61%), Memphis, Tennessee (61%), and Washington, D.C. (60%).

The nation's most affluent county with an African American majority is Prince George's County, Maryland, with a median income of $62,467. Within that county, among the wealthiest communities are Glenn Dale, Maryland and Fort Washington, Maryland. Other affluent predominantly African American counties include Dekalb County in Georgia, and Charles City County in Virginia. Queens County, New York is the only county with a population of 65,000 or more where African Americans have a higher median household income than Americans of European descent.

Religion

Main articles: Black church, Nation of Islam, and Black Hebrew Israelites

The majority of African Americans are Protestant of whom many follow the historically black churches. Black church refers to churches which minister predominantly African American congregations. Black congregations were first established by freed slaves at the end of the 17th century, and later when slavery was abolished more African Americans were allowed to create a unique form of Christianity that was culturally influenced by African spiritual traditions.

Mount Zion United Methodist Church is the oldest African American congregation in Washington, D.C.

According to a 2007 survey, more than half of the African American population are part of the historically black churches. The largest Protestant denomination among African Americans are the Baptists, distributed in four denominations, the largest being the National Baptist Convention and the National Baptist Convention of America. The second largest are the Methodists, the largest sects are the African Methodist Episcopal Church and the African Methodist Episcopal Zion Church. Pentecostals are mainly part of the Church of God in Christ. About 16% of African American Christians are members of white Protestant communions, these denominations (which include the United Church of Christ) mostly have a 2 to 3% African American membership. The are also large numbers of Roman Catholics, constituting 5% of the African American population. Of the total number of Jehovah's Witnesses, 22% are black.

Malcolm Shabazz Mosque in Harlem, New York City

Some African Americans also practice Islam. Historically, between 15 to 30% of enslaved Africans brought to the Americas were Muslims, but most of these Africans were converted to Christianity during the era of American slavery. However during the 20th century, some African Americans converted to Islam, mainly through the influence of black nationalist groups that preached with distinctive Islamic practices; these include the Moorish Science Temple of America, though the largest organization was the Nation of Islam, founded during the 1930s, which attracted at least 20,000 people as of 1963, prominent members included activist Malcolm X and boxer Muhammad Ali.

Malcolm X is considered the first person to start the movement among African Americans towards mainstream Islam, after he left the Nation and made the pilgrimage to Mecca. In 1975, Warith Deen Mohammed, the son of Elijah Muhammad who took control of the Nation after his death, guided majority of its members to orthodox Islam. However, few members rejected these

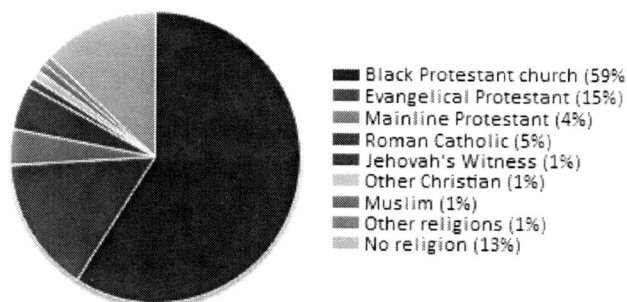

Religious affiliation of African Americans.

changes, in particular Louis Farrakhan, who revived the Nation of Islam in 1978 based on its original teachings.

African American Muslims constitute 20% of the total U.S. Muslim population, the majority are Sunni or orthodox Muslims, some of these identify under the community of W. Deen Mohammed. The Nation of Islam led by Louis Farrakhan has a membership from 20,000—50,000 members. Most of today's growth in blacks practicing Islam has been fueled by an increasing number of African immigrants, particularly from the Horn of Africa who practice the religion. There has also been a high number of converts in prisons.

There are relatively few African American Jews; estimates of their number range from 20,000 to 200,000. Most of these Jews are part of mainstream groups such as the Reform, Conservative, or Orthodox branches of Judaism; although there are significant numbers of people who are part of non-mainstream Jewish groups, largely the Black Hebrew Israelites, whose beliefs include the claim that African Americans are descended from the Biblical Israelites.

Contemporary issues

African Americans have improved their social and economic standing significantly since the Civil Rights Movement and recent decades have witnessed the expansion of a robust, African American middle class across the United States. Unprecedented access to higher education and employment in addition to representation in the highest levels of American government has been gained by African Americans in the post-civil rights era.

Nevertheless, due in part to the legacy of slavery, racism and discrimination, African Americans as a group remain at a pronounced economic, educational and social disadvantage in many areas relative to European Americans. Persistent social, economic and political issues for many African Americans include inadequate health care access and delivery; institutional racism and discrimination in housing, education, policing, criminal justice and employment; crime, poverty and substance abuse.[citation

needed]

One of the most serious and long standing issues within African American communities is poverty. Poverty itself is a hardship as it is related to marital stress and dissolution, health problems, low educational attainment, deficits in psychological functioning, and crime. In 2004, 24.7% of African American families lived below the poverty level. In 2007, the average African American income was $33,916, compared with $54,920 for whites.

Politics and social issues

President Barack Obama at White House Easter Egg Roll.

Collectively, African Americans are more involved in the American political process than other minority groups in the United States, indicated by the highest level of voter registration and participation in elections among these groups in 2004. African Americans collectively attain higher levels of education than immigrants to the United States. African Americans also have the highest level of Congressional representation of any minority group in the U.S.

African Americans tend to vote overwhelmingly for Democrats in U.S. elections. Even most conservative African Americans tend to vote for Democrats[*citation needed*]. In the 2004 Presidential Election, Democrat John Kerry received 88% of the African American vote compared to 11% for Republican George W. Bush. Although there is an African-American lobby in foreign policy, it has not had the impact that African American organizations have had in domestic policy.

Historically, African Americans were supporters of the Republican Party because it was Republican President Abraham Lincoln who helped in granting freedom to American slaves; at the time, the Republicans and Democrats represented the sectional interests of the North and South, respectively, rather than any specific ideology, and both right and left were represented equally in both parties.

The African American trend of voting for Democrats can be traced back to the 1930s during the Great Depression, when Franklin D. Roosevelt's New Deal program provided economic relief to African Americans; Roosevelt's New Deal coalition turned the Democratic Party into an organization of the working class and their liberal allies, regardless of region. The African American vote became even more solidly Democratic when Democratic presidents John F. Kennedy and Lyndon B. Johnson pushed for civil rights legislation during the 1960s.

After over 50 years, marriage rates for *all* Americans began to decline while divorce rates and out-of-wedlock births have climbed. These changes have been greatest among African Americans. After more than 70 years of racial parity black marriage rates began to fall behind whites. Despite that and heavy Democratic leanings, African Americans favor "traditional American values" about family and marriage.

While 52% of Democrats support same-sex marriage, 30% of black Democrats do. In 2008, though Democrats overwhelmingly voted (64%) against the California ballot proposition banning gay marriage, blacks overwhelmingly approved (70% in favor) it, more than any other racial group. The high-profile candidacy of Barack Obama is credited with increasing black turnout on the bill which has been seen as the crucial difference in its passing.

Blacks also hold far more conservative opinions on abortion, extramarital sex, and raising children out of wedlock than Democrats as a whole. On financial issues, however, African Americans are very much in line with Democrats, generally supporting a more progressive tax structure to provide more services and reduce injustice and as well as more government spending on social services.

News media and coverage

News media coverage of African American news, concerns or dilemmas is inadequate, some activists and academics contend. Activists also contend that the news media present distorted images of African Americans. To combat this African Americans founded their own television networks. Black Entertainment Television, founded by Robert L. Johnson is a network that targets young African Americans and urban audiences in the United States.

BET founder Robert L. Johnson with
former U.S. President George W. Bush.

Most programming on the network consists of rap and R&B music videos and urban-oriented movies and series. Additionally, the channel shows syndicated television series, original programs, and some public affairs programs. On Sunday mornings, BET broadcasts a lineup of network-produced Christian programming; other, non-affiliated Christian programs are also shown during the early morning hours daily. BET is now a global network that reaches 85 million viewers in the Caribbean, Canada, and the United Kingdom.

In addition to BET there is Centric, which is a spin-off cable television channel of BET, created originally as BET on Jazz to showcase jazz music-related programming, especially that of black jazz musicians. Programming since has been expanded to include a block of urban programs as well as some R&B, neo soul, and alternative hip hop, with the focus on jazz reduced to low-profile hours.

TV One is another African American-oriented network and a direct competitor to BET. It targets African American adults with a broad range of programming. The network airs original lifestyle and entertainment-oriented shows, movies, fashion and music programming, as well as classic series such as 227, Good Times, Martin, Boston Public and It's Showtime at the Apollo. The network primarily owned by Radio One. Radio One, Inc., founded and controlled by Catherine Hughes, it is one of the nation's largest radio broadcasting companies and the largest African American-owned radio broadcasting company in the United States.

Other African American networks scheduled to launch in 2009 are the Black Television News Channel founded by former Congressman J. C. Watts and Better Black Television founded by Percy Miller. In June 2009, NBC News launched a new website named The Grio in partnership with the production team that created the black documentary film, Meeting David Wilson. It is the first African American video news site which focuses on underrepresented stories in existing national news. The Grio consists of a broad spectrum of original video packages, news articles, and contributor blogs on topics including breaking news, politics, health, business, entertainment and Black History.

Education

Main article: Education outcomes in the United States by race and other classifications

By 2000, African Americans had advanced greatly. They still lagged overall in education attainment compared to white or Asian Americans, with 14 percent with four year and 5 percent with advanced degrees, though it was higher than for other minorities. African Americans attend college at about half the rate of whites, but at a greater rate than Americans of Hispanic origin. More African American women attend and complete college than men. Black schools for kindergarten through twelfth grade students were common throughout the U.S., and a pattern towards re-segregation is currently occurring across the country.

Charles F. Bolden, Jr. is the current
Administrator of NASA

Historically black colleges and universities remain today which were originally set up when segregated colleges did not admit African Americans. As late as 1947, about one third of African Americans over 65 were considered to lack the literacy to read and write their own names. By 1969, illiteracy as it had been traditionally defined, had been largely eradicated among younger African Americans.

US Census surveys showed that by 1998, 89 percent of African Americans aged 25 to 29 had completed high school, less than whites or Asians, but more than Hispanics. On many college entrance, standardized tests and grades, African Americans have historically lagged behind whites, but some studies suggest that the achievement gap has been closing. Many policy makers have proposed that this gap can and will be eliminated through policies such as affirmative action, desegregation, and multiculturalism.

In Chicago, Marva Collins, an African American educator, created a low cost private school specifically for the purpose of teaching low-income African American children whom the public school system had labeled as being "learning disabled". One article about Marva Collins' school stated,

> Working with students having the worst of backgrounds, those who were working far below grade level, and even those who had been labeled as 'unteachable,' Marva was able to overcome the obstacles. News of third grade students reading at ninth grade level, four-year-olds learning to read in only a few months, outstanding test scores, disappearance of behavioral problems, second-graders studying Shakespeare, and other incredible reports, astounded the public.

During the 2006–2007 school year, Collins' school charged $5,500 for tuition, and parents said that the school did a much better job than the Chicago public school system. Meanwhile, during the 2007–2008 year, Chicago public school officials claimed that their budget of $11,300 per student was not enough.

Economic status

Economically, African Americans have benefited from the advances made during the Civil Rights era, particularly among the educated, but not without the lingering effects of historical marginalization when considered as a whole. The racial disparity in poverty rates has narrowed. The black middle class has grown substantially. In 2000, 47% of African Americans owned their homes. The poverty rate among African Americans has decreased from 26.5% in 1998 to 24.7% in 2004. African Americans are the second largest consumer group in America with a combined buying power of over $892 billion currently and likely over $1.1 trillion by 2012. In 2002 African American owned businesses accounted for 1.2 million of the US's 23 million businesses.

Oprah Winfrey, the wealthiest African American of the 20th century. A pair of economists estimate that Winfrey's endorsement of Barack Obama delivered one million votes for him in the close 2008 Democratic primaries.

In 2004, African American workers had the second-highest median earnings of American minority groups after Asian Americans, and African Americans had the highest level of male-female income parity of all ethnic groups in the United States. Also, among American minority groups, only Asian Americans were more likely to hold white-collar occupations (management, professional, and related fields), and African Americans were no more or less likely than European Americans to work in the service industry. In 2001, over half of African American households of married couples earned $50,000 or more. Although in the same year African Americans were over-represented among the nation's poor, this was directly related to the disproportionate percentage of African American families headed by single women; such families are collectively poorer, regardless of ethnicity.

By 2006, gender continued to be the primary factor in income level, with the median earnings of African American men more than those black and non-black American women overall and in all educational levels. At the same time, among American men, income disparities were significant; the median income of African American men was approximately 76 cents for every dollar of their European American counterparts, although the gap narrowed somewhat with a rise in educational level.

Overall, the median earnings of African American men were 72 cents for every dollar earned of their Asian American counterparts, and $1.17 for every dollar earned by Hispanic men. On the other hand by 2006, among American women with post-secondary education, African American women have made significant advances; the median income of African American women was more than those of their Asian-, European- and Hispanic American counterparts with at least some college education.

African Americans are still underrepresented in government and employment. In 1999, the median income of African American families was $33,255 compared to $53,356 of European Americans. In times of economic hardship for the nation, African Americans suffer disproportionately from job loss and underemployment, with the black underclass being hardest hit. The phrase "last hired and first fired" is reflected in the Bureau of Labor Statistics unemployment figures. Nationwide, the October 2008 unemployment rate for African Americans was 11.1%, while the nationwide rate was 6.5%.

The income gap between black and white families is also significant. In 2005, employed blacks earned only 65% of the wages of whites, down from 82% in 1975. *The New York Times* reported in 2006 that in Queens, New York, the median income among African American families exceeded that of white families, which the newspaper attributed to the growth in the number of two-parent black families. It noted that Queens was the only county with more than 65,000 residents where that was true.

In 1999, the rate of births to unwed African American mothers was estimated by economist Walter E. Williams of George Mason University to be 70%. The poverty rate among single-parent black families was 39.5% in 2005, according to Williams, while it was 9.9% among married-couple black families. Among white families, the comparable rates were 26.4% and 6%.

According to *Forbes* magazine's "wealthiest American" lists, a 2000 net worth of $800 million dollars made Oprah Winfrey the richest African American of the 20th century; by contrast, the net worth of the 20th century's richest American, Bill Gates, who is of European descent, briefly hit $100 billion in 1999. In Forbes' 2007 list, Gates' net worth decreased to $59 billion while Winfrey's increased to $2.5 billion, making her the world's richest black person. Winfrey is also the first African American to make Business Week's annual list of America's 50 greatest philanthropists. BET founder Bob Johnson was also listed as a billionaire prior to an expensive divorce and as of 2009, had an estimated net worth of $550 million. Winfrey remains the only African American wealthy enough to rank among the country's 400 richest people. Some black entrepreneurs use their wealth to create new avenues for both African Americans and new opportunities for American business in general. Examples such as Tyler Perry who created new filming studios in Atlanta, Georgia which makes it possible to film movies and television shows outside of California.

Health

African Americans continue to have lower life expectancies on average than whites in the United States. Even when adjusted for age, African Americans are 1.6 times more likely to die from one of the 10 leading causes of death in the United States than European Americans. However, there is evidence that this may be changing: by 2003, sex had replaced race as the primary factor in life expectancy in the United States, with African American females expected to live longer than European American males born in that year.

Ben Carson (left) being announced as a recipient of the Presidential Medal of Freedom at the White House on June 19, 2008.

In the same year, the gap in life expectancy between American whites (78.0) and blacks (72.8) had decreased to 5.2 years, reflecting a long term trend of this phenomenon. By 2004, "the trend toward convergence in mortality figures across the major race groups also continued", with white–black gap in life expectancy dropping to five years. The current life expectancy of African Americans as a group is comparable to those of other groups who live in countries with a high Human Development Index.

At the same time, the life expectancy gap is affected by collectively lower access to quality medical care. With no system of universal health care, access to medical care in the U.S. generally is mediated by income level and employment status. As a result, African Americans, who have a disproportionate occurrence of poverty and unemployment as a group, are more often uninsured than non Hispanic whites or Asians. For a great many African Americans, healthcare delivery is limited, or nonexistent. And when they receive healthcare, they are more likely than others in the general population to receive substandard, even injurious medical care. African Americans have a higher prevalence of some chronic health conditions.

African Americans are the American ethnic group most affected by HIV and AIDS, according to the Centers for Disease Control and Prevention. Black men are six (6) times more likely to have HIV than white men and black women are nearly eighteen (18) times more likely to have HIV than white women. A 2004 "CDC analysis of MSM in five cities found that while only 18 percent of the HIV-infected white men were unaware of their infections, 67 percent of the infected black men were unaware."

It has been estimated that "184,991 adult and adolescent HIV infections [were] diagnosed during 2001–2005" (1). More than 51 percent occurred among blacks than any other race. Between the ages of 25–44 years 62 percent were African Americans. Dr. Robert Janssen (2007) states, "We have rates of HIV/AIDS among blacks in some American cities that are as high as in some countries in Africa". The rate for African Americans with HIV/AIDS in Washington, D.C. is 3 percent, based on cases reported.

In a New York Times Article, about 50 percent of AIDS-related deaths were African American woman, which accounted for 25 percent of the city's population. In many cases there are a higher proportion of black people being tested than any other racial group. Dr. Janssen goes on by saying "We need to do a better job of encouraging African Americans to test. Studies show that approximately one in five black men between the ages 40 to 49 living in the city is HIV-positive, according to the *TIMES*. Research indicates that African Americans' sexual behavior is no different than any other racial group. Dr. Janssen says "Racial groups tend to have sex with members of their own racial group.[*citation needed*]

Crime also plays a significant role in the racial gap in life expectancy. A report from the U.S. Department of Justice states "In 2005, homicide victimization rates for blacks were 6 times higher than the rates for whites" and "94% of black victims were killed by blacks."

Cultural influence in the United States

Further information: African American culture

From their earliest presence in North America, African Americans have contributed literature, art, agricultural skills, foods, clothing styles, music, language, social and technological innovation to American culture. The cultivation and use of many agricultural products in the U.S., such as yams, peanuts, rice, okra, sorghum, grits, watermelon, indigo dyes, and cotton, can be traced to African and African American influences. Notable examples include George Washington Carver, who created 300 products

The King & Carter Jazzing Orchestra photographed in Houston, Texas, January 1921

from peanuts, 118 products from sweet potatoes, and 75 from pecans; and George Crum, who invented the potato chip in 1853.

African American music is one of the most pervasive African American cultural influences in the United States today and is among the most dominant in mainstream popular music. Hip hop, R&B, funk, rock and roll, soul, blues, and other contemporary American musical forms originated in black communities and evolved from other black forms of music, including blues, doo-wop, barbershop, ragtime, bluegrass, jazz, and gospel music.

African American-derived musical forms have also influenced and been incorporated into virtually every other popular musical genre in the world, including country and techno. African American genres are the most important ethnic vernacular tradition in America, as they have developed independent of

African traditions from which they arise more so than any other immigrant groups, including Europeans; make up the broadest and longest lasting range of styles in America; and have, historically, been more influential, interculturally, geographically, and economically, than other American vernacular traditions.

African Americans have also had an important role in American dance. Bill T. Jones, a prominent modern choreographer and dancer, has included historical African American themes in his work, particularly in the piece "Last Supper at Uncle Tom's Cabin/The Promised Land". Likewise, Alvin Ailey's artistic work, including his "Revelations" based on his experience growing up as an African American in the South during the 1930s, has had a significant influence on modern dance. Another form of dance, Stepping, is an African American tradition whose performance and competition has been formalized through the traditionally black fraternities and sororities at universities.[citation needed]

Many African American authors have written stories, poems, and essays influenced by their experiences as African Americans. African-American literature is a major genre in American literature. Famous examples include Langston Hughes, James Baldwin, Richard Wright, Zora Neale Hurston, Ralph Ellison, Nobel Prize winner Toni Morrison, and Maya Angelou.

African American inventors have created many widely used devices in the world and have contributed to international innovation. Norbert Rillieux created the technique for converting sugar cane juice into white sugar crystals. Moreover, Rillieux left Louisiana in 1854 and went to France, where he spent ten years working with the Champollions deciphering Egyptian hieroglyphics from the Rosetta Stone. Most slave inventors were nameless, such as the slave owned by the Confederate President Jefferson Davis who designed the ship propeller used by the Confederate navy.

Chuck Berry in Örebro, Berry is considered a pioneer of American Rock and roll

By 1913 over 1,000 inventions were patented by black Americans. Among the most notable inventors were Jan Matzeliger, who developed the first machine to mass-produce shoes, and Elijah McCoy, who invented automatic lubrication devices for steam engines. Granville Woods had 35 patents to improve electric railway systems, including the first system to allow moving trains to communicate. Garrett A. Morgan developed the first automatic traffic signal and gas mask.

Lewis Howard Latimer invented an improvement for the incandescent light bulb. More recent inventors include McKinley Jones, who invented the movable refrigeration unit for food transport in trucks and trains. Lloyd Quarterman worked with six other black scientists on the creation of the atomic bomb (code named the Manhattan Project.) Quarterman also helped develop the first nuclear reactor, which was used in the atomically powered submarine called the Nautilus.

A few other notable examples include the first successful open heart surgery, performed by Dr. Daniel Hale Williams, the air conditioner, patented by Frederick McKinley Jones. Dr. Mark Dean holds three of the original nine patents on the computer on which all PCs are based. More current contributors include Otis Boykin, whose inventions included several novel methods for manufacturing electrical components that found use in applications such as guided missile systems and computers, and Colonel Frederick Gregory, who was not only the first black astronaut pilot but the person who redesigned the cockpits for the last three space shuttles. Gregory was also on the team that pioneered the microwave instrumentation landing system. In 2000, Bendix Aircraft Company began a worldwide promotion of this microwave instrumentation landing system.

B.B. King is a blues guitarist and songwriter acclaimed for his expressive singing and guitar playing.

Political legacy

African Americans have fought in every war in the history of the United States.

The gains made by African Americans in the Civil Rights and Black Power movements not only obtained certain rights for African Americans, but changed American society in far-reaching and fundamentally important ways. Prior to the 1950s, Black Americans in the South were subject to de jure discrimination, or Jim Crow. They would often be the victims of extreme cruelty and violence, sometimes resulting in deaths: by the post WWII era, African Americans became increasingly discontented with their long-standing inequality. In the words of Martin Luther King, Jr., African Americans and their supporters challenged the nation to "rise up and live out the true meaning of its creed that all men are created equal ..."

Dr. Martin Luther King, Jr. remains the most prominent political leader in the American civil rights movement and perhaps the most influential African American political figure in general.

The Civil Rights Movement marked a sea-change in American social, political, economic and civic life. It brought with it boycotts, sit-ins, demonstrations, court battles, bombings and other violence; prompted worldwide media coverage and intense public debate; forged enduring civic, economic and religious alliances; and disrupted and realigned the nation's two major political parties.

Over time, it has changed in fundamental ways the manner in which blacks and whites interact with and relate to one another. The movement resulted in the removal of codified, *de jure* racial segregation and discrimination from American life and law, and heavily influenced other groups and movements in struggles for civil rights and social equality within American society, including the Free Speech Movement, the disabled, women, Native Americans, and migrant workers.

The term "African American"

Political overtones

Michelle Robinson Obama is the First Lady of the United States, the first African American to hold the position

The term African American carries important political overtones. Earlier terms used to identify Americans of African ancestry were conferred upon the group by colonists and Americans of European ancestry. The terms were included in the wording of various laws and legal decisions which some thought were being used as tools of white supremacy and oppression. There developed among blacks in America a growing desire for a term of self-identification of their own choosing.

With the political consciousness that emerged from the political and social ferment of the late 1960s and early 1970s, blacks no longer approved of the term Negro. They believed it had suggestions of a moderate, accommodationist, even "Uncle Tom" connotation. In this period, a growing number of blacks in the United States, particularly African American youth, celebrated their blackness and their historical and cultural ties with the African continent. The Black Power movement defiantly embraced *Black* as a group identifier. It was a term social leaders themselves had repudiated only two decades earlier, but they proclaimed, "Black is beautiful".

In this same period, a smaller number of people favored *Afro-American*, a common shortening (as is 'Anglo-American'). However, after the demise in popularity of the 'Afro' hairstyle in the late 1970s, many blacks began to be offended by the term 'Afro-American' because of the comical association[*citation needed*].

In the 1980s the term *African American* was advanced on the model of, for example, German-American or Irish-American to give descendents of American slaves and other American blacks who lived through the slavery-era a heritage and a cultural base. The term was popularized in black communities around the country via word of mouth and ultimately received mainstream use after Jesse Jackson publicly used the term in front of a national audience, subsequently major media outlets adopted its use.

Many blacks in America expressed a preference for the term, as it was formed in the same way as names for others of the many ethnic groups in the nation. Some argued further that, because of the historical circumstances surrounding the capture, enslavement and systematic attempts to de-Africanize blacks in the United States under chattel slavery, most African Americans are unable to trace their ancestry to a specific African nation; hence, the entire continent serves as a geographic marker.

For many, African American is more than a name expressive of cultural and historical roots. The term expresses pride in Africa and a sense of kinship and solidarity with others of the African diaspora—an embrace of pan-Africanism as earlier enunciated by prominent African thinkers such as Marcus Garvey, W. E. B. Du Bois and George Padmore.

Who is African American?

Further information: Multiracial American, Mulatto, and Black Indians

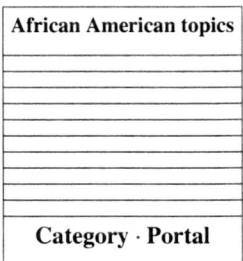

Since 1977, in an attempt to keep up with changing social opinion, the United States government officially classified black people (revised to *black* or *African American* in 1997) as *A person having origins in any of the black racial groups of Africa*. Other Federal offices, such as the United States Census Bureau, adheres to the OMB standards on race in its data collection and tabulations efforts. In preparation for the United States 2010 Census, a marketing and outreach plan, called *2010 Census Integrated Communications Campaign Plan* (ICC) recognized and defined African Americans as black people born in the United States. From the ICC perspective, African Americans are one of three groups of black people in the United States

The ICC plan was to reach the three groups by acknowledging that each group has its own sense of community that is based on geography and ethnicity. The best way to market the census process toward any of the three groups is to reach them through their own unique communication channels and not treat the entire black population of the U.S. as though they are all African Americans with a single ethnic and geographical background. The U.S. Department of Justice Federal Bureau of Investigation categorizes black or African American people as "A person having origins in any of the black racial groups of Africa" through racial categories used in the UCR Program adopted from the Statistical Policy Handbook (1978) and published by the Office of Federal Statistical Policy and Standards, U.S. Department of Commerce, derived from the 1977 OMB classification.

Admixture

On census forms, the government depends on individuals' self-identification. Due in part to a centuries-old history within the United States, historical experiences pre- and post-slavery, and migrations throughout North America, contemporary African Americans possess varying degrees of admixture with European ancestry. A lesser percentage also have Native American ancestry.

With the help of geneticists, the historian Henry Louis Gates, Jr. put African American ancestry in these terms:

- 58 percent of African Americans have at least 12.5 percent European ancestry (equivalent of one great-grandparent);
- 19.6 percent of African Americans have at least 25 percent European ancestry (equivalent of one grandparent);
- 1 percent of African Americans have at least 50 percent European ancestry (equivalent of one parent); and
- 5 percent of African Americans have at least 12.5 percent Native American ancestry (equivalent to one great-grandparent).

However, studies by historians and geneticists show that African Americans have significant Native American heritage due to many different circumstances in different families. African Americans with Native American ancestry have either been accused of not having Native American ancestry or having little native ancestry. One reason being, the genetic tests done to test for how much Indian Blood a person has does not present a complete picture, as argued by geneticists, because tests trace only one bloodline and thus exclude most ancestors.

The short series *African American Lives* which was hosted by historian Henry Louis Gates, Jr. was greatly criticized because the program did not acknowledge nor inform those that were tested that not all ancestry may show up in the tests, especially for those who claimed having Native American heritage.

The most numerous families of free African Americans in the Upper South by the end of the 18th century were descended from white women, free or servant, and African men, slaves, free or indentured servants, who worked and lived closely together during the colonial period in Virginia. Their free descendants migrated to the frontier of Virginia, North Carolina, and South Carolina in the 18th and 19th centuries. There were also similar free families in Delaware and Maryland, as documented by Paul Heinegg.

In their attempt to ensure white supremacy, in the early 20th century some southern states created laws defining a person as black if the person had any known African ancestry. This was a stricter interpretation than what had prevailed earlier and went against commonly accepted social rules of judging a person by appearance. It became known as the one-drop rule, meaning that a single drop of "black blood" made a person "black". Some courts called it the traceable amount rule. Anthropologists called it the hypodescent rule, meaning that racially mixed persons were assigned the status of the subordinate group.

Prior to the one-drop rule, different states had different laws regarding color. More importantly, social acceptance often played a bigger role in how a person was perceived and how identity was construed than any law. In frontier areas there were fewer questions about origins, and the community looked at how people performed, whether they served in the militia and voted. When questions about racial identity arose because of inheritance issues, for instance, litigation outcomes often were based on how people were accepted by neighbors.

In Virginia prior to 1920, for example, a person was legally black if he or she had at least one-eighth black ancestry. The one-drop rule originated in some Southern United States in the late 19th century, likely in response to whites' attempt to limit black political power following the Democrats' regaining control of state legislatures in the late 1870s. The first year in which the U.S. Census did not count mulattoes separately was 1920, evidencing a shift in the American conception of what an African American is.

For African Americans, the one-drop system of pigmentocracy became a significant factor in ethnic solidarity. The binary division of society by race forced African Americans to share more of a common lot in society than they might have after the Civil War, given widely varying ancestry, educational and economic levels. The binary division altered the separate status of the traditionally free people of color in Louisiana, for instance, although they maintained a strong Louisiana Créole culture related to French culture and language, and practice of Catholicism. African Americans began to create common cause—regardless of their multiracial admixture or social and economic stratification. In further changes, during the Civil Rights and Black Power movements, the African American community increased its own pressure for people of any portion of African descent to be claimed solely by the black community.

By the 1980s, parents of mixed-race children (and adults of mixed-race ancestry) began to organize and lobby for the ability to show more than one ethnic category on Census and other legal forms. They refused to be put into just one category. When the U.S. government proposed the addition of the category of "bi-racial" or "multiracial" in 1988, the response from the general public was mostly negative. Some African American organizations and political leaders, such as Senator Diane Watson and Representative Augustus Hawkins, were particularly vocal in their rejection of the category. They feared a loss in political and economic power if African Americans abandoned their one category.

This reaction is characterized as "historical irony" by Daniel (2002). The African American self-designation had been a response to the one-drop rule, but then people resisted the chance to claim their multiple heritages. At the bottom was a desire not to lose political power of the larger group. Whereas before people resisted being characterized as one group regardless of ranges of ancestry, now some of their own were trying to keep them in the same group.

The African-American Experience

Some black scholars have argued that the term "African-American" should refer strictly to the descendents of West or Central African slaves and free people of color who survived the slavery-era, and not the sons and daughters of black immigrants who lack that ancestry. The argument being that grouping all blacks together regardless of their unique ancestral circumstances would inevitably deny the lingering effects of slavery with in the American slave descendent community, in addition to denying black immigrants recognition of their own unique ancestral backgrounds.

In the book *The End of Blackness* published by author Debra Dickerson, she warned against drawing favorable cultural implications from Obama's political rise: "Lumping us all together," Dickerson claimed it, "erases the significance of slavery and continuing racism while giving the appearance of progress." On the liberal website Salon Dickerson wrote, "African-American", in our political and social vocabulary, means those descended from West African slaves, because Obama is not a descendant of West Africans brought involuntarily to the United States as slaves, he is not African-American".

Stanley Crouch wrote in a New York Daily News piece "Obama's mother is of white U.S. stock. His father is a black Kenyan," in a column entitled *What Obama Isn't: Black Like Me*." During the 2008 election African-American columist David Ehrenstein of the LA Times accused white liberals of flocking to Obama because he was a "Magic Negro", a term that refers to a black person with no past who simply appears to assist the mainstream white (as cultural protagonists/drivers) agenda. Ehrenstein went on to say "He's there to assuage white "guilt" they feel over the role of slavery and racial segregation in American history."

Reacting to media criticism of Michelle Obama during the 2008 presidential election, Charles Kenzie Steele, Jr., Southern Christian Leadership Conference CEO said, "Why are they attacking Michelle Obama, and not really attacking, to that degree, her husband? Because he has no slave blood in him." He later claimed it was just meant to be "provocative" but declined to expand on the subject. Former Secretary of State Condolezza Rice (who was famously mistaken for a "recent American immigrant" by French President Nicholas Sarkozy), said "descendants of slaves did not get much of a head start, and I think you continue to see some of the effects of that." She has also rejected an immigrant designation for African-Americans and instead prefers the term "black" or "white" to denote the African and European U.S. founding populations.

Multiculturalism

In recent decades, the multicultural aspect of the United States has continued to expand, in part due to new waves of immigration from Asia, Central and South America, and Africa. Although the terms mixed-race, biracial, and multiracial are increasingly used, it remains common for those who possess visible traits of black heritage to identify or be identified demographically as blacks or African Americans. Socially, some blacks may self-identify by cultural ancestries such as Haitian American or

Nigerian American.

President Obama is sometimes referred to as biracial but self-identifies as black. Tiger Woods embraces a multiracial background which includes his African-American heritage

For example, 55% of European Americans classify President Barack Obama as biracial when they are told that he has a white mother, while 66% of African Americans consider him black. Obama describes himself as black and African American, using both terms interchangeably. Because of that and general conventions, he is generally considered to be African American, if only culturally. African American, bi-racial, and even multiracial are not exclusive categories.

People who are considered African American can also claim Native heritage. Relationships between Native Americans and African slaves first occurred in 1502, and continued throughout the centuries. Tracing the genealogy of African Americans and Native Americans is a difficult process, because records were not kept for most African slaves and many Native Americans did not speak English. Another difficulty is that elder family members sometimes withhold pertinent genealogical information. Knowing a family's geographic origins in different periods is a key factor in helping trace Native American ancestry related to specific tribes.

Native Americans, during the transitional period of Africans becoming the primary race enslaved, were enslaved at the same time and shared a common experience of enslavement. They worked together, lived together in communal quarters, produced collective recipes for food, shared herbal remedies, myths and legends, and in the end they intermarried." In the 18th century, many Native American women did marry freed or runaway African men due to a large decrease in the population of men in Native American villages. In addition, records also show that Native American women actually bought African men, but unknown to European sellers the women freed and married the men into their tribe. It was also beneficial for African men to marry or have children by Native American woman because children born to a mother who was not a slave were free.

In changes of their own, since the 1980s some Native American nations have changed their rules for membership to construe them more narrowly. They have excluded members who also have African American ancestry, or who are descendants of slaves held by the tribe, but without a blood ancestor member of the tribe at certain time periods. After the Civil War, all tribes were supposed to make freed slaves citizens of their tribes, in a pattern similar to freeing slaves held by people in the Confederate states. There has been considerable controversy, for example, over the case of descendants of Cherokee Freedmen, who have recently been expelled from the tribal nation.

Terms no longer in common use

The terms mulatto and colored were widely used until the second quarter of the 20th century, when they were considered outmoded and generally gave way to the use of *negro*. By the 1940s, the term commonly was capitalized, but by the mid 1960s, it had acquired negative connotations, though the term *mulatto* is still in use in many parts of Latin America and is not considered offensive there. Today, in the culture of the United States, the term is considered inappropriate and is now rarely used and perceived as a pejorative.

The term Negro is largely out of use among the younger black generation, but is still used by a substantial block of older black Americans, particularly in the southern U.S. In Latin America, *negro* is the term generally used to refer and describe black people and, similarly to *mulatto*, it is not considered offensive at all in these regions.

Negroid was a term used by anthropologists first in the 18th century to describe some indigenous Africans and their descendants throughout the African diaspora. As with most descriptors of race based on inconsistent, unscientific phenotypical standards,[citation needed] the term is controversial and imprecise.[citation needed] Some blacks have substituted the term Africoid, which, unlike *Negroid*, encompasses the phenotypes of all indigenous peoples of Africa.

See also

- Affirmative action
- African-American art
- African-American history
- African-American literature
- African-American music
- African American Muslims
- African American National Biography Project
- African American Vernacular English
- African American Women, 1960's
- American Black Upper Class
- American Civil War
- Black church
- Black feminism
- Black Loyalist
- Black nationalism
- Military history of African Americans
- Slavery in the United States

Diaspora:

- African Americans in France
- African diaspora
- African immigrants to the United States
- Afro-American
- Afro-Latin American
- American Black Indians
- Americans of Igbo ancestry
- Americo-Liberian
- Black Hispanic and Latino Americans
- Black Nova Scotians
- Black people
- Foreign-born Afro Americans
- Sierra Leone Creole people

Lists:

- Lists of African Americans
- List of African-American-related topics
- List of topics related to Black and African people
- Terminology: Colored, Creole peoples, Negro, Nigger, Nigga

References

- Centerwall, Brandon S. (1984). "Race, socioeconomic status, and domestic homicide, Atlanta, 1971–72.". *American Journal of Public Health* **74** (8): 813–815. doi:10.2105/AJPH.74.8.813 [1].
- Hawkins, Darnell F. (1993). "Inequality, Culture, and Interpersonal Violence". *Health Affairs* **12** (4): 80–95. doi:10.1377/hlthaff.12.4.80 [2].
- Neapolitan, Jerome L. (1998). "Cross-National Variation in Homicide; Is Race A Factor?". *Criminology* **36** (1): 139–156. doi:10.1111/j.1745-9125.1998.tb01243.x [3].
- Bohlen, C. (May 18, 1986). "Does She Say the Same Things in her Native Tongue?". *New York Times*.
- Felder, J. (1992). *From the Statue of Liberty to the Statue of Bigotry*. New York: Jack Felder.
- Felder, J. (July 16, 1990). "Black Origins and Lady Liberty". *Daily Challenge*.
- Sinclair, T. (July 5, 1986). "Was Original Statue a Tribute to Blacks?". *New York Voice*.
- "Statue of Liberty". *New York Post*. June 17, 1986.
- Altman, Susan. *The Encyclopedia of African-American Heritage*.
- Southern, Eileen (1997). *The Music of Black Americans: A History* (3rd ed.). W. W. Norton & Company. ISBN 0393971414.
- Stewart, Earl L. (1998). *African American Music: An Introduction*. ISBN 0028602943.

Further reading

- Jack Salzman, ed., *Encyclopedia of Afro-American culture and history*, New York, New York : Macmillan Library Reference USA, 1996.
- *African American Lives*, edited by Henry L. Gates, Evelyn Brooks Higginbotham, Oxford University Press, 2004—more than 600 biographies.
- *From Slavery to Freedom. A History of African Americans*, by John Hope Franklin, Alfred Moss, McGraw-Hill Education 2001, standard work, first edition in 1947.
- *Black Women in America: An Historical Encyclopedia*, Darlene Clark Hine (Editor), Rosalyn Terborg-Penn (Editor), Elsa Barkley Brown (Editor), Paperback Edition, Indiana University Press 2005.
- Ivan van Sertima, "They Came Before Columbus".
- "The Politicization of Changing Terms of Self Reference Among American Slave Descendants", *American Speech*, v 66, no.2, Summer 1991, pp. 133–46.

External links

- Richard Thompson Ford Name Games [4], *Slate*, September 16, 2004. Article discussing the problems of defining *African American*
- "Of Arms & the Law: Don Kates on Afro-American Homicide Rates" [5]
- *Scientific American* Magazine (June 2006) Trace Elements [6] Reconnecting African-Americans to an ancestral past
- "The Definition of Political Absurdity" [7], *San Francisco Chronicle*, March 2, 2007
- African American archaeology in Sacramento, California [8] pdf
- African American archaeology in Oakland, California [9]—See Part III, Chap 10
- Black History related original documents and photos [10]
- President Obama's Speech to the NAACP on July 16, 2009 [11]—full video by *MSNBC*
- Black or African American? [12], Frank Newport. Gallup, September 28, 2007
- The Long Journey of Black Americans [13] - slideshow by *The First Post*

Woodward High School

Woodward High School may refer to one of several high schools in the United States:

- Woodward High School (Cincinnati, Ohio) — Cincinnati, Ohio
- Woodward High School (Toledo, Ohio) — Toledo, Ohio
- Charles W. Woodward High School — Rockville, Maryland
- Woodward High School (Oklahoma) — Woodward, Oklahoma
- Woodward-Granger High School — Woodward, Iowa

Orthodox stance

An **Orthodox stance** is a way of positioning both the feet and hands in combat sports such as boxing, karate, kick boxing, and mixed martial arts. A traditional orthodox stance is one in which the boxer places his or her left foot farther in front of the right foot, thus having his or her weaker side closer to the opponent. As it favors the stronger, dominant side — often the right side, see laterality — the orthodox stance is the most common stance in boxing. It is mostly used by right-handed boxers. Many boxing champions, such as Marco Antonio Barrera, Rocky Marciano, Floyd Mayweather Jr, Muhammad Ali, Mike Tyson, Lennox Lewis, Wladimir Klitschko , Joe Frazier and Sugar Ray Robinson used an orthodox stance.

Alternative stances

The corresponding designation for a left-handed boxer is southpaw and is generally a mirror-image of the orthodox stance. A southpaw boxer guards and jabs with his right-hand. Some famous boxers who use southpaw are Marvin 'Marvelous' Hagler, Sultan Ibragimov, Naseem Hamed, Joe Calzaghe, David Tua and Manny Pacquiao. In fiction Rocky Balboa was traditionally a southpaw, however switching to an orthodox stance to confuse his opponent at times.

Some fighters are naturally left handed fight in the orthodox stance with the advantage of a fast, hard jab and left hook. Those examples include: Oscar De La Hoya, Miguel Angel Cotto, Marco Antonio Barrera, Nonito Donaire to name a few. Though they are far from common, many gym trainers who lack experience in training lefties tend to convert southpaws to a right handed stance.

External links

- MV Index review of *orthodox stance* [1]

Double bass

Not to be confused with double bass or acoustic bass guitar. For the technique used in percussion, see double bass drum.

String instrument	
	Side and front views of a modern double bass with a French-style bow
Other names	Bass, string bass, upright bass, standup bass, acoustic bass, contrabass, contrabass violin, bass violin, bass viol, bass fiddle, bull fiddle, dog house bass, coffin bass *contrabbasso*.
Classification	String instrument (bowed or plucked)
Hornbostel-Sachs classification	321.322-71 (Composite chordophone sounded by a bow)
Developed	15th century
Playing range	

Related instruments	
	• Viol • Violin • Bass guitar • Acoustic bass guitar • Electric upright bass
Musicians	
	• List of double bassists

The **double bass**, also called the **string bass, upright bass, bass violin** or **contrabass**, is the largest and lowest-pitched bowed string instrument in the modern symphony orchestra. The double bass is a standard member of the string section of the symphony orchestra and smaller string ensembles in Western classical music. In addition, it is used in other genres such as jazz, 1950s-style blues and rock and roll, rockabilly/psychobilly, traditional country music, bluegrass, tango and many types of folk music.

The double bass is typically constructed from several types of wood, including maple for the back, spruce for the top, and ebony for the fingerboard. It is uncertain whether the instrument is a descendant of the viola da gamba or of the violin, but it is traditionally aligned with the violin family. While the double bass is nearly identical in construction to other violin family instruments, it also embodies features found in the older viol family.

Like many other string instruments, the double bass is played either with a bow (arco) or by plucking the strings (pizzicato). In orchestral repertoire and tango music, both arco and pizzicato are employed. In jazz, pizzicato is the norm, except for some solos and also occasional written parts in modern jazz that call for bowing. In most other genres, such as blues and rockabilly, the bass is plucked.

The double bass is a transposing instrument and sounds one octave lower than notated.

History

The double bass is generally regarded as a modern descendant of the string family of instruments that originated in Europe in the 15th century, and as such it has been described as a "bass violin." Before the 20th century many double basses had only three strings, in contrast to the five to six strings typical of instruments in the string family or the four strings of instruments in the violin family. Some existing instruments, such as those by Gasparo da Salò, were converted from 16th-century six-string contrabass violoni.

The double bass's proportions are dissimilar to those of the violin and cello; for example, it is deeper (the distance from top to back is proportionally much greater than the violin). In addition, while the violin has bulging shoulders, most double basses have shoulders carved with a more acute slope, like members of the viol family. Many very old double basses have had their shoulders cut or sloped to aid playing with modern techniques. Before these modifications, the design of their shoulders was closer to instruments of the violin family.

The double bass is the only modern bowed string instrument that is tuned in fourths (like a viol), rather than fifths (see Tuning, below). The issue of the instrument's exact lineage is still a matter of some debate, and the supposition that the double bass is a direct descendant of the viol family is one that has not been entirely resolved.

In his *A New History of the Double Bass*, Paul Brun asserts, with many references, that the double bass has origins as the true bass of the violin family. He states that, while the exterior of the double bass may resemble the viola da gamba, the internal construction of the double bass is nearly identical to instruments in the violin family, and very different from the internal structure of viols.

Terminology

A person who plays this instrument is called a bassist, double bassist, double bass player, contrabassist, contrabass player, or bass player. The names **contrabass** and **double bass** refer the instrument's range and use in the contra octave below the cello, also called the 16' octave relative to the church organ. The terms for the instrument among classical performers are **contrabass** (which comes from the instrument's Italian name, contrabbasso), **string bass** (to distinguish it from a brass bass instrument in a concert band), or simply **bass**.

In jazz and other genre musicians outside of classical music commonly call it the **upright bass** or **acoustic bass** to distinguish it from the electric bass guitar. In folk and bluegrass music, the instrument is also referred to as a bass fiddle or bass violin (or more rarely as doghouse bass or bull fiddle). Other colourful nicknames are found in other languages; in Hungarian, for instance, the double bass is sometimes called *nagy bőgő*, which roughly translates as "big crier", referring to its large voice.

Design

Example of a Busetto-shaped double bass: Copy of a Matthias Klotz (1700) by Rumano Solano

In general there are two major approaches to the design outline shape of the double bass, these being the violin form, and the viol da gamba form. A third less common design called the busetto shape can also be found, as can the even more rare guitar or pear shape. The back of the instrument can vary from being a round, carved back similar to that of the violin, or a flat and angled back similar to the viol family.

The double bass features many parts that are similar to members of the violin family including a bridge, f-holes, a tailpiece, a scroll and a sound post. Unlike the rest of the violin family, the double bass still reflects influence and can be considered partly derived from the viol family of instruments, in particular the violone, the bass member of the viol family.

The double bass also differs from members of the violin family in that the shoulders are (sometimes) sloped, the back is often angled (both to allow easier access to the instrument, particularly in the upper range), and machine tuners are always fitted. Lack of standardization in design means that one double bass can sound and look very different from another.

Construction

The double bass is closest in construction to violins, but has some notable similarities to the violone (literally "large viol"), the largest and lowest member of the viola da gamba family. Unlike the violone, however, the fingerboard of the double bass is unfretted, and the double bass has fewer strings (the violone, like most viols, generally had six strings, although some specimens had five or four).

An important distinction between the double bass and other members of the violin family is the construction of the pegbox. While the violin, viola, and cello all use friction pegs for gross tuning adjustments, the double bass has metal machine heads. The key on the tuning machine turns a metal "worm", which drives a worm gear that winds the string. While this development makes fine tuners unnecessary, a very small number of bassists use them nevertheless. At the base of the double bass is a metal rod with a

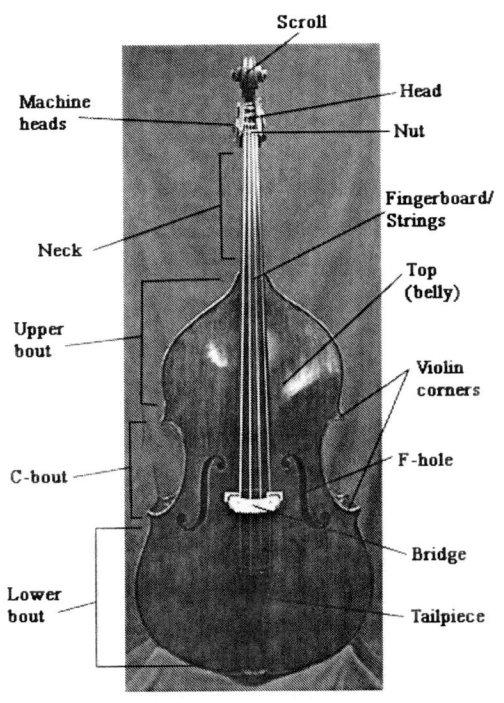

Principal parts of the double bass

spiked end called the endpin, which rests on the floor. This endpin is generally more robust than that of a cello, because of the greater mass of the double bass.

The soundpost and bass bar are components of the internal construction. The materials most often used are maple (back, neck, ribs), spruce (top), and ebony (fingerboard, tailpiece). Exceptions to this include less-expensive basses that have laminated (plywood) tops, backs, and ribs, and some newer mid-range basses made of willow. These basses are resistant to changes in heat and humidity, which can cause cracks in spruce tops. Plywood laminate basses, which are used in music schools, youth orchestras, and in popular and folk music settings, are very resistant to humidity and heat, as well to the physical abuse they are apt to encounter in a school environment (or, for blues and folk musicians, to the hazards of touring and performing in bars).

All the parts of a double bass are glued together, except the soundpost, bridge and tailpiece, which are held in place by string tension, although the soundpost usually remains in place when the instrument's strings are loosened or removed. The metal tuning machines are attached to the sides of the pegbox with metal screws. While tuning mechanisms generally differ from the higher-pitched orchestral stringed instruments, some basses have non-functional, ornamental tuning pegs projecting from the side of the pegbox, in imitation of the tuning pegs on a cello or violin.

Famous double bass makers come from around the world and often represent varied national characteristics. The most highly sought (and expensive) instruments come from Italy and include basses made by Giovanni Paulo Maggini, Gaspar da Salo, the Testore family (Carlo Antonio, Carlo Giuseppe, Gennaro, Giovanni, Paulo Antonio), Celestino Puolotti, and Matteo Gofriller. French and English basses are also sought by players of the highest caliber.

Strings

The history of the double bass is tightly coupled to the development of string technology, as it was the advent of overwound gut strings which first rendered the instrument more generally practicable, as wound strings attain low notes within a smaller overall string diameter than unwound strings.

Detail of the bridge and strings

Prior to the mid-20th century[citation needed], double bass strings were usually made of gut, but since that time, steel strings have largely replaced gut strings, because steel strings hold their pitch better and yield more volume when played with the bow. Gut strings are also more vulnerable to changes of humidity and temperature, and they break much more easily than steel strings. Gut strings are nowadays mostly used by bassists who perform in baroque ensembles, rockabilly bands, traditional blues bands, and bluegrass bands. Gut strings provide the dark, "thumpy" sound heard on 1940s and 1950s recordings. The late Jeff Sarli, a blues upright bassist, stated that "starting in the 1950s, they began to reset the necks on basses for steel strings", and double bass players switched from gut strings to steel strings. Rockabilly and bluegrass bassists also prefer gut because it is much easier to perform the "slapping" upright bass style (in which the strings are percussively slapped and clicked against the fingerboard) with gut strings than with steel strings. (For more information on slapping, see the sections below on Modern playing styles, Double bass in bluegrass music, Double bass in jazz, and Double bass in popular music).

Gut strings

The change from gut to steel has also affected the instrument's playing technique over the last hundred years, because playing with steel strings allows the strings to be set up closer to the fingerboard, and, additionally, steel strings can be played in higher positions on the lower strings and still produce clear tone. The classic 19th century Franz Simandl method does not utilize the low E string in higher positions because with older gut strings set up high over the fingerboard, the tone was not clear in these higher positions. However, with modern steel strings, bassists can play with clear tone in higher positions on the low E and A strings, particularly when modern lighter-gauge, lower-tension steel strings are used.

Bows

The double bass bow comes in two distinct forms (shown below). The "French" or "overhand" bow is similar in shape and implementation to the bow used on the other members of the orchestral string instrument family, while the "German" or "Butler" bow is typically broader and shorter, and is held in a "hand shake" position.

These two bows provide different ways of moving the arm and distributing force on the strings. Proponents of the French bow argue that it is more maneuverable, due to the angle at which the player holds the bow. Advocates of the German bow claim that it allows the player to apply more arm weight on the strings. The differences between the two, however, are minute for a proficient player, and both bows are used by modern players in major orchestras.

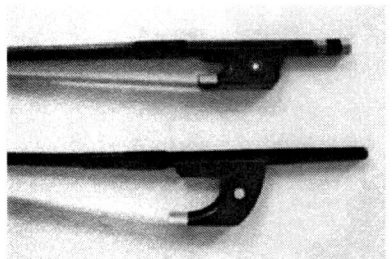

French and German bows compared

German bow

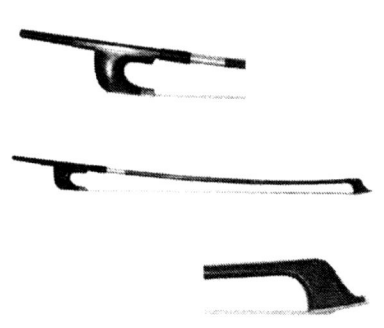

German-style bow

The German bow (sometimes called Dragonetti bow) is the older of the two designs. The design of the bow and the manner of holding it are descended from the older viol family of instruments. With older viols, before screw threads were used to tighten the bow, players held the bow with two fingers between the stick and the hair to maintain tension of the hair . Proponents of the use of German bow claim that the German bow is easier to use for light bow strokes as staccato, spiccato, and detaché[citation needed].

In comparison with the French bow, the German bow has a taller frog, and it is held with the palm angled upwards, as is done for the upright members of the viol family. When held in correct manner, the thumb rests on the side of the stick. The index finger balances the bow at the point where the frog meets the stick. The index finger is also used to apply an upward torque to the frog when tilting the bow. The little finger (or "pinky") supports the frog from underneath, while the ring finger and middle finger are used to apply the force to move the bow across the strings.

French bow

The French bow was not widely popular until its adoption by 19th-century virtuoso Giovanni Bottesini. This style is more similar to the traditional bows of the smaller string family instruments. It is held as if the hand is resting by the side of the performer with the palm facing toward the bass. The thumb rests on the shaft of the bow, next to the frog while the other fingers drape on the other side of the bow. Various styles dictate the curve of the fingers and thumb, as do the style of piece; a more pronounced curve and lighter hold on the bow is used for virtuoso or more delicate pieces, while a flatter curve and sturdier grip on the bow provides more power for loud orchestral passages.

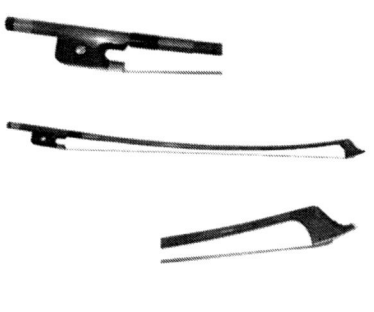

French-style bow

Bow construction and materials

Double bass bows vary in length, ranging from 60 cm (24") to 75 cm (30"). Pernambuco, also known as Brazilwood, is regarded as an excellent quality stick material, but due to its scarcity and expense, other materials are increasingly being used. Less expensive student bows may be constructed of solid fiberglass, or of less valuable varieties of brazilwood. Snakewood and carbon fiber are also used in bows of a variety of different qualities. The frog of the double bass bow is usually made out of ebony, although Snakewood and buffalo horn are used by some luthiers. The wire wrapping is gold or silver in many quality bows, and the hair is usually

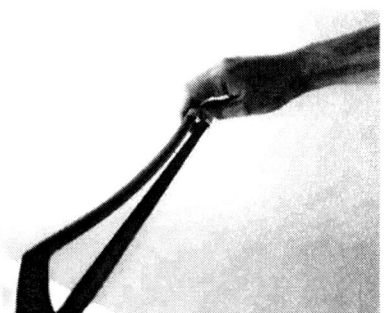

A bassist holding a French bow; note how the thumb rests on the shaft of the bow next to the frog.

horsehair. Some of the lowest-quality student bows are made from molded plastic and synthetic fiberglass "hair".

The double bass bow is strung with either white or black horsehair, or a combination of the two (known as "salt and pepper"), as opposed to the customary white horsehair used on the bows of other string instruments. Some bassists argue that the slightly rougher black hair "grabs" the heavier, lower strings better.[citation needed] As well, some bassists and luthiers believe that it is easier to produce a smoother sound with the white variety. [citation needed]Red hair (chestnut) is also used by some bassists.[citation needed]

Rosin

String players apply rosin to the bow hair so it will "grip" the string and make it vibrate. Double bass rosin is generally softer and stickier than violin rosin to allow the hair to grab the thicker strings better, but players use a wide variety of rosins that vary from quite hard (like violin rosin) to quite soft, depending on the weather, the humidity, and the preference of the player. The amount used generally depends on the type of music being performed as well as the personal preferences of the player. Bassists may apply more rosin in works for large orchestra (e.g., Brahms symphonies) than for delicate chamber works.[citation needed] Some brands of rosin, such as Pop's double bass rosin, are softer and more prone to melting in hot weather. Other brands, such as Carlsson or Nyman Harts double bass rosin, are harder and less prone to melting.[citation needed]

Pitch

The lowest note of a double bass is an E_1 (on standard four-string basses) at approximately 41 Hz or a B0 (when five strings are used) at approximately 31 Hz. This is slightly above the lowest frequency that the average human ear can perceive as a distinctive pitch—about 20 Hz [citation needed]. The top of the instrument's fingerboard range is typically near the G two octaves above the open pitch of the G string as shown in the range illustration found at the head of this article.

The bass (or F) clef is used for most orchestral double bass music.

Many double bass symphony parts and virtuoso concertos employ harmonics (also called flageolet tones). Both natural harmonics and artificial harmonics, where the thumb stops the note and the octave or other harmonic is activated by lightly touching the string at the relative node point, extend the instrument's range considerably.

Orchestral parts rarely demand the double bass exceed a three-octave range (an example of an exception to this rule is Orff's Carmina Burana, which calls for three octaves and a perfect fourth). However, there is no hard limit to the upper range a virtuoso solo player can achieve using natural and artificial harmonics. The high harmonic in the range illustration found at the head of this article may be taken as representative rather than normative.

Five-string instruments have an additional string typically tuned to a low B below the E string. Occasionally, a higher string is added instead, tuned to the C above the G string.

Four-string instruments may feature the C extension extending the range of the E string downwards to C.

Double bass is a transposing instrument. Since the range of the double bass lies largely below the standard bass clef, it is notated an octave higher than it sounds. This transposition applies even when reading the tenor and treble clef, which are used to avoid excessive ledger lines when notating the instrument's upper range.

Tuning

The double bass is generally tuned in fourths, in contrast to members of the orchestral string family, which are tuned in fifths. Modern double basses are usually tuned, low to high, E-A-D-G, which is one octave lower than the four lowest-pitch strings on a guitar.

Throughout classical repertoire, there are notes that fall below the range of a standard double bass. Notes below low E appear regularly in the double bass parts found in later arrangements and interpretations of Baroque music. These parts are transpositions of parts written for other bass instruments used before the modern double bass became common and may actually lower the part an octave.

In the Classical era the double bass typically doubled the cello part an octave below, occasionally requiring descent to C below the E of the four-string double bass. In the Romantic era and the 20th-century, composers such as Mahler, Beethoven, Busoni, and Prokofiev also requested notes below the low E. There are two common methods for making these notes available to the player. Major European orchestras generally use basses with a fifth string, tuned to B three octaves and a semitone below middle C. Players with standard double basses (E-A-D-G) typically play the notes below "E" an octave higher.

In the United States, Canada and United Kingdom, most professional orchestral players use four-string double basses with a "C extension", which extends the lowest string down as far as low C, an octave below the lowest note on the cello (more rarely, this string may be tuned to a low B). The extension is an extra section of fingerboard mounted up over the head of the bass. There are several varieties of extensions.

In the simplest mechanical extensions, there are no mechanical aids attached to the fingerboard extension except a locking nut for the "E" note. To play the extension notes, the player reaches back over the pegs to

A low-C extension with wooden mechanical "fingers" that can be used to stop the string at C#, D, Eb, or E.

press the string to the fingerboard. The advantage of this "fingered" extension is that the player can adjust the intonation of all of the stopped notes on the extension, and there are no mechanical noises from metal keys and levers. The disadvantage of the "fingered" extension is that it can be hard to perform rapid alternations between low notes on the extension and notes on the regular fingerboard, such as a bassline that quickly alternates between "G" and the low "D".

The simplest type of mechanical aid is the use of wooden "fingers" that can be closed to press the string down and fret the C#, D, Eb, or E notes. This system is particularly useful for basslines that have a repeating pedal point such as a low D, because once the note is locked in place with the mechanical "finger", the lowest string then sounds a different note when it is played "open" (e.g., a low D).

The most complicated mechanical aid for use with extensions are mechanical lever systems nicknamed "machines". These lever systems, which superficially resemble the mechanisms of reed instruments such as the bassoon, include levers mounted beside the regular fingerboard (near the nut, on the "E" string side), which remotely activate metal "fingers" on the extension fingerboard. The most expensive metal lever systems also give the player the ability to "lock" down notes on the extension fingerboard, as with the wooden "finger" system. One criticism of these devices is that they may lead to unwanted metallic clicking noises.

A small number of bass players tune their strings in fifths, like a cello but an octave lower (C-G-D-A low to high). This tuning was used by the jazz player Red Mitchell and is increasingly used by classical players, notably the Canadian bassist Joel Quarrington. In classical solo playing the double bass is usually tuned a whole tone higher (F♯-B-E-A). This higher tuning is called "solo tuning", whereas the regular tuning is known as "orchestral tuning." String tension differs so much between solo and orchestral tuning that a different set of strings is often employed that has a lighter gauge. Strings are always labelled for either solo or orchestral tuning, and published solo music is arranged for either solo or orchestral tuning. Some popular solos and concerti, such as the *Koussevitsky Concerto* are available in both solo and orchestral tuning arrangements.

A variant and much less-commonly used form of solo tuning used in some Eastern European countries is (A-D-G-C), which uses three of the strings from orchestral tuning (A-D-G) and then adds a high "C" string. Some bassists with five-string basses use a high "C" string as the fifth string, instead of a low "B" string. Adding the high "C" string facilitates the performance of solo repertoire with a high tessitura (range). Another option is to utilize both a low C (or B) extension and a high C string.

When choosing a bass with a fifth string, the player must decide between adding a higher or lower-tuned string. Six-stringed instruments are generally regarded as impractical. To accommodate the additional string, the fingerboard is usually slightly wider, and the top slightly thicker to handle the increased tension. Some five-stringed instruments are converted four-string instruments. Because these don't have wider fingerboards, some players find them more difficult to finger and bow. Converted four-string basses usually require either a new, thicker top, or lighter strings to compensate for the increased tension.

Playing and performance considerations

Body and hand position

Double bassists either stand or sit to play the instrument. When standing, the double bass' height is set (by adjusting the endpin) so that the player may easily place the right hand close to the bridge, either with the bow (arco) or plucking (pizzicato). While personal opinions vary, often the endpin is set by aligning the first finger in either first or half position with the player's eye level. While sitting, a stool (measured by the player's pants inseam length) is used. Traditionally, standing has been preferred by soloists although many now choose to play sitting down. Proponents of playing while sitting on a stool argue that it is easier to perform high-register passages, because they can steady the instrument between the knees.

When playing in the instrument's upper range (above the G below middle C), the player shifts his hand out from behind the neck and flattens it out, using the side of the thumb to press down the string. This technique—also used on the cello—is called *thumb position*. While playing in thumb position, most players do not use the fourth (little) finger, as it is too weak to produce a reliable tone (this is also true for cellists).

Physical considerations

Performing on bass can be physically demanding because the strings are large and thick. Also, the space between notes on the fingerboard is large due to the scale length and string spacing, so players have to shift positions frequently. The bass is usually discouraged for people with shorter arms and smaller hands due to the big note gaps and the thick strings. The increased use of playing techniques such as thumb position and modifications to the bass, such as the use of lighter-gauge strings at lower tension, have eased the difficulty of playing the instrument. Bass parts have relatively fewer fast passages, double stops, or large jumps in range. These parts are usually given to the cello section due to the fact that it is a smaller instrument and are typically tuned together.

As with all non-fretted string instruments, performers must learn to place their fingers precisely to produce the correct pitch. The more frequent hand movement required by the instrument's size increases the likelihood of intonation errors. For bassists with smaller hands, the large spaces between pitches may present a significant challenge, especially in the lowest range, where the spaces between notes are largest.

Until the 1990s, child-sized double basses were not widely available, and the large size of the bass meant that children were not able to start playing the instrument until their hand size and height would allow them to play a 3/4-size model (the most commonly available size). Starting in the 1990s, smaller half, quarter, eighth and even sixteenth-sized instruments became more widely available, which meant that children could start at a younger age.

Volume

Despite the size of the instrument, it is not as loud as many other instruments due to its low range. In a large orchestra, usually between four and eight bassists play in unison. In the largest orchestras, bass sections may have as many as ten or twelve players, but modern budget constraints make bass sections this large unusual.

When writing solo passages for the bass in orchestral or chamber music, composers typically ensure the orchestration is light so it doesn't obscure the bass. While amplification is rarely used in classical music, in some cases where a bass soloist performs a concerto with a full orchestra, subtle amplification called acoustic enhancement may be used. The use of microphones and amplifiers in a classical setting has led to debate within the classical community, as "...purists maintain that the natural acoustic sound of [Classical] voices [or] instruments in a given hall should not be altered."

In many non-orchestral settings, such as jazz and blues, amplification via a specialized amplifier and loudspeakers is employed. Bluegrass and jazz players typically use less amplification than blues, psychobilly, or jam band players. In the latter cases, the high overall volume due to other amplifiers and instruments may lead to acoustic feedback, a problem exacerbated by the bass's large surface area and interior volume. The feedback problem has led to the development of instruments like the electric upright bass, whose playing characteristics mimic that of the double bass.

Transportation

The double bass's large size and relative fragility make it cumbersome to handle and transport. Most bassists use soft cases, referred to as gig bags, to protect the instrument during transport. Basic, unpadded gig bags used by students cost under 100 USD, while thickly padded gig bags for professional players typically cost as much as 500 USD. Some more feature-filled examples with backpack straps retail for over 1000 USD. Some bassists carry their bow in a hard bow case. Players also may use a small cart or gig bag and end pin-attached wheels to move the bass.

Hard flight cases have cushioned interiors and tough exteriors of carbon fiber, graphite, fiberglass, or Kevlar. The cost of good hard cases—USD 500 to over USD 2500—tends to limit their use to touring professionals.

Classical repertoire

Solo works for double bass

1700s

The double bass as a solo instrument enjoyed a period of popularity during the 18th century and many of the most popular composers from that era wrote pieces for the double bass. The double bass, then often referred to as the Violone used different tunings from region to region. The "Viennese tuning" (A^1-D-F♯-A) was popular, and in some cases a fifth string or even sixth string was added (F^1-A^1-D-F♯-A). The popularity of the instrument is documented in Leopold Mozart's second edition of his Violinschule, where he writes "One can bring forth difficult passages easier with the five-string violone, and I heard unusually beautiful performances of concertos, trios, solos, etc."

The earliest known concerto for double bass was written by Joseph Haydn ca.1763, and is presumed lost in a fire at the Eisenstadt library. The earliest known existing concertos are by Karl Ditters von Dittersdorf, who composed two concertos for the double bass and a Sinfonia Concertante for viola and double bass. Other composers that have written concertos from this period include Johann Baptist Vanhal, Franz Anton Hoffmeister (3 concertos), Leopold Kozeluch, Anton Zimmermann, Antonio Capuzzi, Wenzel Pichl (2 concertos), and Johannes Matthias Sperger (18 concertos). While many of these names were leading figures to the music public of their time, they are generally unknown by contemporary audiences. Wolfgang Amadeus Mozart's concert aria, "Per Questa Bella Mano", K.612 for bass, double bass obbligato, and orchestra contains impressive writing for solo double bass of that period. It remains popular among both singers and double bassists today.

The double bass eventually evolved to fit the needs of orchestras that required lower notes and a louder sound. The leading double bassists from the mid-to-late 18th century, such as Josef Kämpfer, Friedrich Pischelberger, and Johannes Mathias Sperger employed the "Viennese" tuning. Bassist Johann Hindle (1792–1862), who composed a concerto for the double bass, pioneered tuning the bass in fourths, which marked a turning point for the double bass and its role in solo works. Bassist Domenico Dragonetti was a prominent musical figure and an acquaintance of Haydn and Ludwig van Beethoven. His playing was known all the way from his homeland Italy to the Tsardom of Russia and he found a prominent place performing in concerts with the Philharmonic Society of London.

Beethoven's friendship with Dragonetti may have inspired him to write difficult, separate parts for the double bass in his symphonies, such as the impressive passages in the third movement of the Fifth Symphony and last movement of the Ninth Symphony. These parts do not double the cello part. Dragonetti wrote ten concertos for the double bass and many solo works for bass and piano. During Rossini's stay in London in the summer of 1824, he composed his Duetto for cello and double bass for Dragonetti and the cellist David Salomons. Dragonetti frequently played on a three string double bass tuned G-D-A from top to bottom. The use of only the top three strings was popular for bass soloists and Principal bassists in orchestras in the 19th century, because it reduced the pressure on the wooden top of the bass, which was thought to create a more resonant sound. As well, the low "E" strings used during the 19th century were thick cords made of gut, which were difficult to tune and play.

The Italian bass virtuoso Domenico Dragonetti helped to encourage composers to give more difficult parts for his instrument.

1800s

In the 19th century, the opera conductor, composer, and bassist Giovanni Bottesini was considered the "Paganini of the double bass" of his time. His compositions were written in the popular Italian opera style of the 19th century, which exploit the double bass in a way that was not seen beforehand. They require virtuosic runs and great leaps to the highest registers of the instrument, even into the realm of harmonics. These compositions were considered to be unplayable by many bassists in the early part of the 20th century, but are now frequently performed. During the same time, a prominent school of bass players in the Czech region arose, which included Franz Simandl, Theodore Albin Findeisen, Josef Hrabe, Ludwig Manoly, and Adolf Mišek. Simandl and Hrabe were also pedagogues whose method books and studies continue to be used in modern times.

1900s-present

The leading figure of the double bass in the early 20th century was Serge Koussevitzky, best known as conductor of the Boston Symphony Orchestra, who popularized the double bass in modern times as a solo instrument. Because of improvements to the double bass with steel strings and better set-ups, the bass is now played at a more advanced level than ever before and more and more composers have written works for the double bass. In the mid-century and in the following decades, many new concerti were written for the double bass, including Nikolaos Skalkottas's Concerto (1942), Eduard Tubin's Concerto (1948), Lars-Erik Larsson's Concertino (1957), Gunther Schuller's Concerto (1962), and Hans

Werner Henze's Concerto (1966).

From the 1960s through the end of the century Gary Karr was the leading proponent of the double bass as a solo instrument and was active in commissioning or having hundreds of new works and concerti written especially for him. Karr was given Koussevitzky's famous solo doublebass by Olga Koussevitsky and played it in concerts around the world for 40 years before, in turn, giving the instrument to the International Society of Bassists for talented soloists to use in concert.

In the 1970s and 1980s, new concerti included Nino Rota's *Divertimento for Double Bass and Orchestra* (1973), Jean Françaix's Concerto (1975), Einojuhani Rautavaara's *Angel Of Dusk* (1980), Gian Carlo Menotti's Concerto (1983), Christopher Rouse's Concerto (1985), and Henry Brant's Ghost Nets (1988). In the first decade of the 21st century, new concerti include Kalevi Aho's Concerto (2005), John Harbison's *Concerto for Bass Viol* (2006), and André Previn's Double Concerto for violin, double bass, and orchestra (2007).

Serge Koussevitzky popularized the double bass in modern times as a solo instrument

Reinhold Glière wrote and Intermezzo and Tarantella for double bass and piano, Op. 9, No. 1 and No. 2 and a Praeludium and Scherzo for double bass and piano, Op. 32 No.1 and No.2. Paul Hindemith wrote a rhythmically challenging Double Bass Sonata in 1949. Giacinto Scelsi wrote two double bass pieces called *Nuits* in 1972, and then in 1976, he wrote *Maknongan*, a piece for any low-voiced instrument, such as double bass, contrabassoon, or tuba. Vincent Persichetti wrote solo works—which he called "Parables"—for many instruments. He wrote Parable XVII for Double Bass, Op. 131 in 1974. Sofia Gubaidulina penned a Sonata for double bass and piano in 1975. In 1977 Dutch-Hungarian composer Geza Frid wrote a set of variations on The Elephant from Saint-Saëns' Le Carnaval des Animaux for scordatura Double Bass and string orchestra. In 1987 Lowell Liebermann wrote his Sonata for Contrabass and Piano Op.24. Fernando Grillo wrote the "Suite No.1" for double bass (1983/2005). Jacob Druckman wrote a piece for solo double bass entitled *Valentine*. US double bass soloist and composer Bertram Turetzky (born 1933) has performed and recorded more than 300 pieces written by and for him. He writes chamber music, baroque music, classical, jazz, renaissance music, improvisational music and world music

US minimalist composer Philip Glass wrote a prelude focused on the lower register that he scored for timpani and double bass. Italian composer Sylvano Bussotti, whose composing career spans from the 1930s to the first decade of the 21st century, wrote a solo work for bass in 1983 entitled *Naked Angel Face per contrabbasso*. Fellow Italian composer Franco Donatoni wrote a piece called *Lem for contrabbasso* in the same year. In 1989, French composer Pascal Dusapin (born 1955) wrote a solo piece called *In et Out* for double bass. In 1996, the Sorbonne-trained Lebanese composer Karim Haddad composed *Ce qui dort dans l'ombre sacrée* ("He who sleeps in the sacred shadows") for Radio France's Presence Festival. Renaud Garcia-Fons (born 1962) is a French double-bass player and composer, notable for drawing on jazz, folk, and Asian music for recordings of his pieces like *Oriental Bass* (1997). Two significant recent works written for solo bass include, Mario Davidovsky's Synchronisms No.11 for double bass and electronic sounds and Elliott Carter's Figment III, for solo double bass.

Chamber music with double bass

Since there is no established instrumental ensemble that includes the double bass, its use in chamber music has not been as exhaustive as the literature for ensembles such as the string quartet or piano trio. Despite this, there is a substantial number of chamber works that incorporate the double bass in both small and large ensembles.

There is a small body of works written for piano quintet with the instrumentation of piano, violin, viola, cello, and double bass. The most famous is Franz Schubert's Piano Quintet in A major, known as "The Trout Quintet" for its set of variations in the fourth movement of Schubert's "Die Forelle". Other works for this instrumentation written from roughly the same period include those by Johann Nepomuk Hummel, George Onslow, Jan Ladislav Dussek, Louise Farrenc, Ferdinand Ries, Franz Limmer, Johann Baptist Cramer, and Hermann Goetz. Later composers who wrote chamber works for this quintet include Ralph Vaughan Williams, Colin Matthews, Jon Deak, Frank Proto, and John Woolrich. Slightly larger sextets written for piano, string quartet, and double bass have been written by Felix Mendelssohn, Mikhail Glinka, Richard Wernick, and Charles Ives.

In the genre of string quintets, there are a few works for string quartet with double bass. Antonín Dvořák's String Quintet in G major, Op.77 and Wolfgang Amadeus Mozart's Serenade in G major, K.525 ("Eine kleine Nachtmusik") are the most popular pieces in this repertoire, along with works by Darius Milhaud, Luigi Boccherini (3 quintets), Harold Shapero, and Paul Hindemith. Slightly smaller string works with the double bass include six string sonatas by Gioachino Rossini, for two violins, cello, and double bass written at the age of twelve over the course of three days in 1804. These remain his most famous instrumental works and have also been adapted for wind quartet.

Larger works that incorporate the double bass include Beethoven's Septet in E-flat major, Op.20, one of his most famous pieces during his lifetime, which consists of clarinet, horn, bassoon, violin, viola, cello, and bass. When the clarinetist Ferdinand Troyer commissioned a work from Franz Schubert for similar forces, he added one more violin for his Octet in F major, D.803. Paul Hindemith used the same instrumentation as Schubert for his own Octet. In the realm of even larger works, Mozart included the double bass in addition to 12 wind instruments for his "Gran Partita" Serenade, K.361 and Martinů used the double bass in his nonet for wind quintet, violin, viola, cello and double bass.

Other examples of chamber works that use the double bass in mixed ensembles include Serge Prokofiev's Quintet in G minor, Op.39 for oboe, clarinet, violin, viola, and double bass; Erwin Schulhoff's Concertino for flute/piccolo, viola, and double bass; Fred Lerdahl's Waltzes for violin, viola, cello, and double bass; Mario Davidovsky's Festino for guitar, viola, cello, and double bass; and Iannis Xenakis's Morsima-Amorsima for piano, violin, cello, and double bass.

Orchestral passages and solos

The double bass in the baroque and classical periods would typically double the cello part in orchestral passages. A notable exception would be Haydn, who composed solo passages for the double bass in his Symphonies No.6 "Le Matin", No.7 "Le midi", No.8 "Le Soir", No. 31 "Horn Signal, and No. 45 "Farewell", but who otherwise would group the bass and cello parts together. Beethoven paved the way for separate double bass parts, which became more common in the romantic era. The scherzo and trio from Beethoven's Fifth Symphony are famous orchestral excerpts, as is the recitative at the beginning of the fourth movement of Beethoven's Ninth Symphony.

While orchestral bass solos are somewhat rare, there are some notable examples. Johannes Brahms, whose father was a double bass player, wrote many difficult and prominent parts for the double bass in his symphonies. Richard Strauss assigned the double bass daring parts, and his symphonic poems and operas stretch the instrument to its limits. "The Elephant" from Camille Saint-Saëns' *The Carnival of the Animals* is a satirical portrait of the double bass, and American virtuoso Gary Karr made his televised debut playing "The Swan" (originally written for the cello) with the New York Philharmonic conducted by Leonard Bernstein. The third movement of Gustav Mahler's first symphony features a solo for the double bass that quotes the children's song "Frere Jacques", transposed into a minor key. Sergei Prokofiev's "Lieutenant Kijé Suite" features a difficult and very high double bass solo in the "Romance" movement. Benjamin Britten's *The Young Person's Guide to the Orchestra* contains a prominent passage for the double bass section.

Double bass ensembles

Ensembles made up entirely of double basses, though relatively rare, also exist, and several composers have written or arranged for such ensembles. Compositions for four double basses exist by Gunther Schuller, Jacob Druckman, James Tenney, Robert Ceely, Jan Alm, Bernhard Alt, Frank Proto, Joseph Lauber, Erich Hartmann, and Theodore Albin Findeisen. Bertold Hummel wrote a *Sinfonia piccola* [1] for eight double basses. Larger ensemble works include Galina Ustvolskaya's Composition No. 2, "Dies Irae" (1973), for eight double basses, piano, and wooden cube, Jose Serebrier's George and Muriel (1986), for solo bass, double bass ensemble, and chorus, and Gerhard Samuel's *What of my music!* (1979), for soprano, percussion, and 30 double basses.

Active double bass ensembles include L'Orchestre de Contrebasses (6 members), Bass Instinct (6 members), Bassiona Amorosa (6 members), the Chicago Bass Ensemble (4+ members), The Bass Gang

(4 members), the London Double Bass Ensemble (6 members) founded by members of the Philharmonia Orchestra of London who produced the LPMusic Interludes by London Double Bass Ensemble [2] on Bruton Music records, and the ensembles of Ball State University (12 members) and the Hartt School of Music. The Amarillo Bass Base of Amarillo, Texas once featured 52 double bassists, and The London Double Bass Sound, who have released a CD on Cala Records, have 10 players.

In addition, the double bass sections of some orchestras perform as an ensemble, such as the Chicago Symphony Orchestra's Wacker Consort. There is an increasing number of published compositions and arrangements for double bass ensembles, and the International Society of Bassists regularly features double bass ensembles (both smaller ensembles as well as very large "mass bass" ensembles) at its conferences, and sponsors the biennial David Walter Composition Competition, which includes a division for double bass ensemble works.

Use in jazz

See also List of jazz bassists (which includes both upright bass and electric bass guitar players)

Beginning around 1890, the early New Orleans jazz ensemble (which played a mixture of marches, ragtime, and Dixieland) was initially a marching band with a tuba or sousaphone (or occasionally bass saxophone) supplying the bass line. As the music moved into bars and brothels, the double bass gradually replaced these wind instruments. Many early bassists doubled on both the "brass bass" and "string bass", as the instruments were then often referred to. Bassists played "walking" bass lines—scale-based lines that outlined the harmony.

Because an unamplified upright bass is generally the quietest instrument in a jazz band, many players of the 1920s and 1930s used the *slap style*, slapping and pulling the strings so that they make a rhythmic "slap" sound against the fingerboard. The slap style cuts through the sound of a band better than simply plucking the strings, and allowed the bass to be more easily heard on early sound recordings, as the recording equipment of that time did not favor low frequencies. For more about the slap style, see "Modern playing styles", below.

Many string bass players have contributed to the evolution of jazz. Examples include swing era players such as Jimmy Blanton, who played with Duke Ellington, and Oscar Pettiford, who pioneered the instrument's use in bebop. Paul Chambers (who worked with Miles Davis on the famous *Kind of Blue* album) achieved renown for being one of the first jazz bassists to play bebop solos with the bow. Charlie Haden, best known for his work with Ornette Coleman, defined the role of the bass in Free Jazz.

A number of other bassists, such as Niels-Henning Ørsted Pedersen, Ray Brown and Slam Stewart, were central to the history of jazz. Notably, Charles Mingus was a highly regarded composer as well as a bassist noted for his technical virtuosity and powerful sound. Scott LaFaro influenced a generation of musicians by liberating the bass from contrapuntal "walking" behind soloists instead favoring interactive, conversational melodies.

Monk Montgomery (brother of guitarist Wes Montgomery) is perhaps the first electric bassist of significance in jazz, introducing the Fender Precision Bass to the genre in 1951. Miles Davis began incorporating bass guitar in his music on the album "Miles In the Sky" (1968), featuring Ron Carter on the instrument. Beginning in the 1970s bassist Bob Cranshaw, playing with saxophonist Sonny Rollins, and fusion pioneers Jaco Pastorius and Stanley Clarke began to substitute the electric bass guitar for the upright bass. Apart from the jazz styles of jazz fusion and Latin-influenced jazz, the upright bass is still widely used in jazz. The sound and tone of the

Jazz bassist Charles Mingus was also an influential bandleader and composer whose musical interests spanned from bebop to free jazz.

plucked upright bass is distinct from that of the fretted bass guitar. The bass guitar produces a different sound than the upright bass, because its strings are usually stopped with the aid of metal frets. As well, bass guitars usually have a solid wood body, which means that the sound is produced by electronic amplification of the vibration of the strings.

Use in bluegrass and related genres

The string bass is the most commonly used bass instrument in bluegrass music and is almost always plucked, though some modern bluegrass bassists have also used a bow. The bluegrass bassist is part of the rhythm section, and is responsible for keeping a steady beat, whether fast, slow, in 4/4 time, 2/4 or 3/4 time. The Englehardt and Kay brands of laminate basses have long been popular choices for bluegrass bassists. Most bluegrass bassists use the 3/4 size bass, but the full-size and 5/8 size basses are also used.

Upright bass used by a bluegrass group; the
cable for a piezoelectric pickup can be seen
extending from the bridge.

Early pre-bluegrass traditional music was often accompanied by the cello. The cellist Natalie Haas points out that in the US, you can find "... old photographs, and even old recordings, of American string bands with cello." However, "the cello dropped out of sight in folk music and became associated with the orchestra". The cello did not reappear in bluegrass until the 1990s and first decade of the 21st century. Some contemporary bluegrass bands favor the electric bass, because it is easier to transport than the large and somewhat fragile upright bass. However, the bass guitar has a different musical sound. Many musicians feel the slower attack and percussive, woody tone of the upright bass gives it a more "earthy" or "natural" sound than an electric bass, particularly when gut strings are used.

Common rhythms in bluegrass bass playing involve (with some exceptions) plucking on beats 1 and 3 in 4/4 time; beats 1 and 2 in 2/4 time, and on the downbeat in 3/4 time (waltz time). Bluegrass bass lines are usually simple, typically staying on the root and fifth of each chord throughout most of a song. There are two main exceptions to this "rule". Bluegrass bassists often do a diatonic "walkup" or "walkdown" in which they play every beat of a bar for one or two bars, typically when there is a chord change. In addition, if a bass player is given a solo, they may play a walking bass line with a note on every beat or play a pentatonic scale-influenced bassline.

An early bluegrass bassist to rise to prominence was Howard Watts (also known as Cedric Rainwater), who played with Bill Monroe's Blue Grass Boys beginning in 1944. The classical bassist Edgar Meyer has frequently branched out into newgrass, old-time, jazz, and other genres. "My all-time favorite is Todd Phillips", proclaimed Union Station bassist Barry Bales in April 2005. "He brought a completely different way of thinking about and playing bluegrass.

Country music bassist "Too Slim" (Fred LaBour of Riders in the Sky) performing in Ponca City, Oklahoma in 2008.

An upright bass was the standard bass instrument in traditional country western music. While the upright bass is still occasionally used in country music, the electric bass has largely replaced its bigger cousin in country music, especially in the more pop-infused country styles of the 1990s and 2000s, such as new country.

Slap-style bass

Slap-style bass is sometimes used in bluegrass bass playing. When bluegrass bass players slap the string by pulling it until it hits the fingerboard or hit the strings against the fingerboard, it adds the high-pitched percussive "clack" or "slap" sound to the low-pitched bass notes, sounding much like the clacks of a tap dancer. Slapping is a subject of minor controversy in the bluegrass scene. Even slapping experts such as Mike Bub say, "...don't slap on every gig" or in songs where it is "not appropriate." As well, bluegrass bassists who play slap-style on live shows often slap less on records. Bub and his mentor Jerry McCoury rarely do slap bass on recordings. While bassists such as Jack Cook slap bass "...on the occasional faster Clinch Mountain boys song", bassists such as "...Gene Libbea, Missy Raines, Jenny Keel, or Barry Bales [rarely] slap bass."

Bluegrass bassist Mark Schatz, who teaches slap bass in his *Intermediate Bluegrass Bass* DVD acknowledges that slap bass "...has not been stylistically very predominant in the music I have recorded." He notes that "Even in traditional bluegrass slap bass only appears sporadically and most of what I've done has been on the more contemporary side of that (Tony Rice, Tim O'Brien)." Schatz states that he would be "... more likely to use it [slap] in a live situation than on a recording — for a solo or to punctuate a particular place in a song or tune where I wouldn't be obliterating someone's solo.". Another bluegrass method, *Learn to Play Bluegrass Bass*, by Earl Gately, also teaches bluegrass slap bass technique.

Use in popular music

In 1952, the upright bass was a standard instrument in rock and roll music, Marshall Lytle of Bill Haley & His Comets being but one example. In the 1940s, a new style of dance music called rhythm and blues developed, incorporating elements of the earlier styles of blues and swing. Louis Jordan, the first innovator of this style, featured a upright bass in his group, the Tympany Five. The upright bass remained an integral part of pop lineups throughout the 1950s, as the new genre of rock and roll was built largely upon the model of rhythm and blues, with strong elements also derived from jazz, country, and bluegrass. However, upright bass players using their instruments in these contexts faced inherent problems. They were forced to compete with louder horn instruments (and later amplified electric guitars), making bass parts difficult to hear. The upright bass is difficult to amplify in loud concert venue settings, because it can be prone to feedback "howls". The upright bass is large and

Double bass player from the Bunjevac minority group in Hungary.

awkward to transport, which also created transportation problems for touring bands. In some groups, the slap bass was utilized as band percussion in lieu of a drummer; such was the case with Bill Haley & His Saddlemen (the forerunner group to the Comets), which did not use drummers on recordings and live performances until late 1952; prior to this the slap bass was relied on for percussion, including on recordings such as Haley's versions of Rock the Joint and Rocket 88.

In 1951, Leo Fender independently released his Precision Bass, the first commercially successful electric bass guitar. The electric bass was easily amplified with its built-in pickups, easily portable (less than a foot longer than an electric guitar), and easier to play in tune, thanks to the metal frets. In the 1960s and 1970s bands were playing at louder volumes and performing in larger venues. The electric bass was able to provide the huge, highly amplified stadium-filling bass tone that the pop and rock music of this era demanded, and the upright bass receded from the limelight of the popular music scene.

The upright bass began making a modest comeback in popular music in the mid-1980s, in part due to a renewed interest in earlier forms of rock and country music. In the 1990s, improvements in pickups and amplifier designs for electro-acoustic horizontal and upright basses made it easier for bassists to get a good, clear amplified tone from an acoustic instrument. Some popular bands decided to anchor their sound with an upright bass instead of an electric bass. A trend for "unplugged" performances further helped to enhance the public's interest in the upright bass and acoustic bass guitars.

The bassist for psychobilly band The HorrorPops, seen here at a 2006 show, uses a colorful, custom-painted upright bass with a cutaway upper shoulder for easier access to the higher positions.

Peter Steele, bassist/vocalist for the gothic metal band Type O Negative, was renown for occasionally playing an upright bass held like a guitar. This feat was made possible only by his considerable height (6'8").

The upright bass is also favored over the electric bass guitar in many rockabilly and psychobilly bands. In such bands the bassist often plays with great showmanship, using slapping technique, sometimes spinning the bass around or even physically climbing onto the instrument while performing; this style was pioneered c. 1953 by Marshall Lytle, the bassist for Bill Haley & His Comets, and modern performers of such stunts include Lee Rocker of the Stray Cats, Phil Bloomberg of The Polecats, Scott Owen from The Living End and Jimbo from Reverend Horton Heat. Primus's Les Claypool used an upright bass for the song "Mr. Krinkle", from Pork Soda, and for the song "Over the Falls", from the *Brown Album*.

Shannon Burchell, of the Australian folk-rock group The John Butler Trio, makes extensive use of upright basses, performing extended live solo's in songs such as Betterman. On the 2008 album In Ear Park by the indie/pop band Department of Eagles, a bowed upright bass is featured quite prominently on the songs "Teenagers" and "In Ear Park". Norwegian ompa-rock band Kaizers Orchestra use the upright bass exclusively both live and on their recordings.

Hank Williams II's bass players (Joe Buck and Zach Shedd,most notably) have used upright basses for recording as well as during the country and Hellbilly sets of Hank III's live performances before switching to electric bass for the Assjack set.

Modern playing styles

In popular music genres, the instrument is usually played with amplification and almost exclusively played with the fingers, *pizzicato* style. The pizzicato style varies between different players and genres. Some players perform with the sides of one, two, or three fingers, especially for walking basslines and slow tempo ballads, because this is purported to create a stronger and more solid tone. Some players use the more nimble tips of the fingers to play fast-moving solo passages or to pluck lightly for quiet tunes.The use of amplification allows the player to have more control over the tone of the instrument, because amplifiers have equalization controls that allow the bassist to accentuate certain frequencies (often the bass frequencies) while de-accentuating some frequencies (often the high frequencies, so that there is less finger noise).

An unamplified acoustic bass' tone is limited by the frequency responsiveness of the instrument's hollow body, which means that the very low pitches may not be as loud as the higher pitches. With an amplifier and equalization devices, a bass player can boost the low frequencies, which evens out the frequency response. As well, the use of an amplifier can increase the sustain of the instrument, which is particularly useful for accompaniment during ballads and for melodic solos with held notes.

In traditional jazz, swing, polka, rockabilly, and psychobilly music, it is sometimes played in the *slap style*. This is a vigorous version of pizzicato where the strings are "slapped" against the fingerboard between the main notes of the bass line, producing a snare drum-like percussive sound. The main notes are either played normally or by pulling the string away from the fingerboard and releasing it so that it bounces off the fingerboard, producing a distinctive percussive attack in addition to the expected pitch. Notable slap style bass players, whose use of the technique was often highly syncopated and virtuosic, sometimes interpolated two, three, four, or more slaps in between notes of the bass line.

"Slap style" may have influenced electric bass guitar players who from the mid-sixties (particularly Larry Graham of Sly and the Family Stone) developed a technique called "slap and pop", where the thumb of the plucking hand is used to hit the string, making a slapping sound but still allowing the note to ring, and the index or middle finger of the plucking hand is used to pull the string back so it hits the fretboard, achieving the pop sound described above.

Double bassists

Historical

- Domenico Dragonetti (1763–1846) Virtuoso, composer, conductor
- Giovanni Bottesini (1821–1889) Virtuoso, composer, conductor
- Franz Simandl (1840–1912) Virtuoso, composer, pedagogue
- Edouard Nanny (1872–1943) Virtuoso, composer
- Serge Koussevitzky (1874–1951) Virtuoso, composer, conductor

Contemporary (1900s-present)

Classical

Some of the most influential contemporary classical double bass players are known as much for their contributions to pedagogy than for their performing skills, such as US bassist Oscar G. Zimmerman (1910–1987), known for his teaching at the Eastman School of Music and, for 44 summers at the Interlochen National Music Camp in Michigan and French bassist François Rabbath (b. 1931) who developed a new bass method that divided the entire fingerboard into six positions. Bassists noted for their virtuoso solo skills include Canadian player Gary Karr (b. 1941), Finnish composer Teppo Hauta-Aho (b. 1941), Italian composer Fernando Grillo, and US player-composer Edgar Meyer. For a longer list, see the *List of contemporary classical double bass players*.

Double bass soloist Gary Karr

Jazz

Notable jazz bassists from the 1940s to the 1950s included bassist Jimmy Blanton (1918–1942) whose short tenure in the Duke Ellington Swing band (cut short by his death from tuberculosis) introduced new melodic and harmonic solo ideas for the instrument; bassist Ray Brown (1926–2002), known for backing Beboppers Dizzy Gillespie, Oscar Peterson, Art Tatum and Charlie Parker, and forming the Modern Jazz Quartet; hard bop bassist Ron Carter (born 1937), who has appeared on 3,500 albums make him one of the most-recorded bassists in jazz history, including LPs by Thelonious Monk and Wes Montgomery and many Blue Note Records artists; and Paul Chambers (1935–1969), a member of the Miles Davis Quintet (including the landmark modal jazz recording *Kind of Blue*) and many other 1950s and 1960s rhythm sections, was known for his virtuosic improvisations.

In the experimental post 1960s eras, which saw the development of free jazz and jazz-rock fusion, some of the influential bassists included Charles Mingus (1922–1979), who was also a composer and bandleader whose music fused hard bop with black gospel music, free jazz and classical music; free jazz and post-bop bassist Charlie Haden (born 1937) is best known for his long association with saxophonist Ornette Coleman and for his role in the 1970s-era Liberation Music Orchestra, an experimental group; and fusion virtuoso Stanley Clarke (born 1951) is notable for his dexterity on both the upright bass and the electric bass. In the 1990s and first decade of the 21st century, one of the new "young lions" was Christian McBride (born 1972), who has performed with a range of veterans ranging from McCoy Tyner to fusion gurus Herbie Hancock and Chick Corea, and who has released albums such as 2003's *Vertical Vision*. For a longer list, see the List of jazz bassists, which includes both double bass and electric bass players.

Other popular genres

In addition to being a noted classical player, Edgar Meyer is well-known in bluegrass and newgrass circles. Todd Phillips is another prominent bluegrass player. Well-known rockabilly bassists include Bill Black, Marshall Lytle (with Bill Haley & His Comets) and Lee Rocker (with 1980s-era rockabilly revivalists the Stray Cats). Notable rockabilly revivalists and psychobilly performers from the 1990s and first decade of the 21st century include Scott Owen (from the Australian band The Living End), Jimbo Wallace (from the US band Reverend Horton Heat), Kim Nekroman (Nekromantix), Patricia Day (HorrorPops), Geoff Kresge (Tiger Army, ex-AFI). Willie Dixon (1915–1992) was one of the most notable figures in the history of rhythm and blues. In addition to being an upright bassist, he wrote dozens of R&B hits and worked as a producer. He also plays bass on numerous Chuck Berry's rock and roll hits. Many other rockabilly bands like El Rio Trio (from the Netherlands) also use this instrument in their work.

Pedagogy and training

The pedagogy and training for the double bass varies widely by genre and country. Classical double bass has a history of pedagogy dating back several centuries, including teaching manuals, studies, and progressive exercises that help students to develop the endurance and accuracy of the left hand, and control for the bowing hand. Classical training methods vary by country: many of the major European countries are associated with specific methods (e.g., the Edouard Nanny method in France or the Franz Simandl method in Germany). In Classical training, the majority of the instruction for the right hand focuses on the production of bowing tone; little time is spent studying the varieties of pizzicato tone.

In contrast, in genres that mainly or exclusively use pizzicato (plucking), such as jazz and blues, a great deal of time and effort is focused on learning the varieties of different pizzicato styles used for music of different styles of tempi. For example, in jazz, aspiring bassists have to learn how to perform a wide range of pizzicato tones, including using the sides of the fingers to create a full, deep sound for ballads, using the tips of the fingers for fast walking basslines or solos, and performing a variety of percussive "ghost notes" by "raking" muted or partially muted strings.

Formal training

Of all of the genres, Classical and jazz have the most established and comprehensive systems of instruction and training. In the Classical milieu, children can begin taking private lessons on the instrument and performing in children's or youth orchestras. Teens who aspire to becoming professional Classical bassists can continue their studies in a variety of formal training settings, including colleges, conservatories, and universities. Colleges offer certificates and diplomas in bass performance.

Spalding performing on December 10, 2009 at the Nobel Peace Price Concert of 2009

Manhattan School of Music professor Timothy Cobb teaching a bass lesson in the late 2000s

Conservatories, which are the standard musical training system in France and in Quebec (Canada) provide lessons and amateur orchestral experience for double bass players. Universities offer a range of double bass programs, including Bachelor's degrees, Master of Music degrees, and Doctor of Musical Arts degrees. As well, there are a variety of other training programs such as Classical summer camps and orchestral, opera, or chamber music training festivals, which give students the opportunity to play a wide range of music.

Bachelor's degrees in bass performance (referred to as B.Mus. or B.M) are four-year programs that include individual bass lessons, amateur orchestra experience, and a sequence of courses in music history, music theory, and liberal arts courses (e.g., English literature), which give the student a more well-rounded education. Usually, bass performance students perform several recitals of solo double bass music, such as concertos, sonatas, and Baroque suites.

Master of music degrees in double bass performance consist of private lessons, ensemble experience, coaching in playing orchestral double bass parts, and graduate courses in music history and music theory, along with one or two solo recitals. A Master's degree in music (referred to as an M.Mus. or M.M.) is often a required credential for people who wish to become a professor of double bass at a university or conservatory.

Doctor of Musical Arts (referred to as D.M.A., DMA, D.Mus.A. or A.Mus.D) degrees in double bass performance provide an opportunity for advanced study at the highest artistic and pedagogical level, requiring usually an additional 54+ credit hours beyond a Master's degree (which is about 30+ credits beyond a Bachelor's degree). For this reason, admission to candidacy is highly selective. Examinations in music history, music theory, ear training/dictation, plus an entrance examination/recital, are required to enter such a program of study. A number of recitals (around six), including a lecture-recital for which an accompanying doctoral dissertation is submitted, advanced coursework and a minimum B average are other typical requirements of a D.M.A program.

Throughout the early history of jazz, double bass players either learned the instrument informally, or from getting Classical training early on, as in the case of Ron Carter and Charles Mingus. In the 1980s and 1990s, colleges and universities began to introduce diplomas and degrees in jazz performance. Students in jazz diploma or Bachelor of Music programs take individual bass lessons, get experience in small jazz combos with coaching from an experienced player, and play in jazz big bands. As with Classical training programs, jazz programs also include classroom courses in music history and music theory. In a jazz program, these courses focus on the different eras of jazz history. such as Swing, Bebop, and fusion. The theory courses focus on the musical skills used in jazz improvisation and in jazz "comping" (accompanying) and the composition of jazz tunes. There are also jazz summer camps and training festivals/seminars, which offer students the chance to learn new skills and styles.

Informal training

In other genres, such as blues, rockabilly, and psychobilly, the pedagogical systems and training sequences are not as formalized and institutionalized. There are not degrees in blues bass performance, or conservatories offering multiple-year diplomas in rockabilly bass. However, there are a range of books, playing methods, and, since the 1990s, instructional DVDs (e.g., on how to play rockabilly-style slap bass). As such, performers in these other genres tend to come from a variety of routes, including informal learning by using bass method books or DVDs, taking private lessons and coaching, and learning from records and CDs. In some cases, blues or rockabilly bassists may have obtained some initial training through the Classical or jazz pedagogy systems (e.g., youth orchestra or high school big band). In genres such as tango, which use a lot of bowed passages and jazz-style pizzicato lines. the bassists tend to come from Classical or jazz training routes.

Careers

Careers in double bass vary widely by genre and by region or country. Most bassists earn their living from a mixture of performance and teaching jobs. The first step to getting most performance jobs is by playing at an audition. In some styles of music, such as jazz-oriented stage bands, bassists may be asked to sight read printed music or perform standard pieces (e.g., a jazz standard such as "Now's the Time") with an ensemble. Similarly, in a rock or blues band, auditionees may be asked to play various rock or blues standards. An upright bassist auditioning for a blues band might be asked to play in a Swing-style walking bassline, a rockabilly-style "slapping" bassline (in which the strings are percussively struck against the fingerboard) and a 1950s ballad with long held notes. A person auditioning for a role as a bassist in some styles of pop or rock music may be expected to be able to demonstrate the ability to perform harmony vocals as a backup singer.

In Classical music, bassists do auditions to get playing jobs in orchestras and to get into university or Conservatory programs or degrees. At a Classical bass audition, the performer typically plays a movement from a Bach suite or a movement from a bass concerto and a variety of excerpts from the orchestral literature. Orchestral bass auditions are typically held in front of a panel that includes the conductor, the Concertmaster, the Principal bass player, and possibly other principal players such as the Principal cellist. The most promising candidates are invited to return for a second or third round of auditions, which allows the conductor and the panel to compare the best candidates. Performers may be asked to sight read orchestral music. The final stage of the audition process in some orchestras is a "test week", in which the performer plays with the orchestra for a week or two, which allows the conductor and Principal players to see if the individual can function well in an actual performance setting.

Performance jobs include playing as a freelancer in small groups, large ensembles, or performing solo music, either live onstage or as a "session player" for radio or TV broadcasts or for recordings; and working as the employee of an orchestra, big band, or recording studio (as the studio's "house bassist"). Many bass players find extra work by substituting ("subbing") for bassists who are double-booked or ill. It is hard for bass players to be able to find full-time, full-year work at a single job. About the closest that a bass player can come to this is in the case of Classical bass players who win an audition at a professional orchestra or the tiny number of top session pros that are hired by recording studios. Even full-time orchestra jobs do not usually last for the entire year. When the orchestra stops playing (which is often in the summer), orchestral bassists have to find other work, either as a teacher or coach, or in another group.

Some bassists supplement their income by working as an instrument repairperson.

Teaching work for double bassist includes giving private lessons in the home or at colleges and universities; coaching bass players who are preparing for recordings or auditions; doing group coaching at music camps or for youth ensembles; and working as a high school music teacher.

In jazz, blues, rockabilly and other genres, most bassists cannot earn a living from playing in a single group (with the exception of a the small number of bassists in top touring bands or groups with recording contracts), so they work in different bands, and supplement their income with session playing and teaching. Due to the limited number of full-time orchestral jobs, many Classical bassists are similarly not able to find full-time work with a single orchestra. Some bassists increase their employability by learning several different styles, such as Classical and jazz or rockabilly and bluegrass.

In some cases, bassists supplement their performing and teaching income with other related music jobs, such as working as a bass repairer (luthier); acting as a contractor who hires musicians for orchestras or big bands. composing music (e.g., Dave Holland), songwriting, conducting (e.g., David Currie), or acting as a bandleader (e.g., Charles Mingus). In some regions, there may not be enough work in music to make a living, even if a bassist can play several styles and he or she does recordings and teaching. As such, in some regions, bassists may have to supplement their musical work with income from another field outside of music.

See also

- Electric upright bass
- List of jazz bassists
- List of historical classical double bass players
- List of contemporary classical double bass players
- List of double bass concerti
- Octobass
- Piccolo bass
- *Bach: Unaccompanied Cello Suites Performed on Double Bass*
- International Society of Bassists
- Bazantar

External links

- Bass [3] at the Open Directory Project
- EarlyBass.com by Jerry Fuller [4]

Burr Oak Cemetery

Burr Oak Cemetery is a 150-acre (0.61 km^2) cemetery located in unincorporated Cook County, Illinois, adjacent to Alsip, a suburb slightly southwest of Chicago. Many musicians from the Chicago blues era are buried here.

On July 9, 2009 Cook County Sheriff Tom Dart alleged that four workers at Burr Oak cemetery dug up more than 200 graves, dumped the bodies into unmarked mass graves, and resold the plots in a scheme that went back at least five years. The three men and one woman were charged with one count each of dismembering a human body.

Because of the investigation, the entire cemetery was declared a crime scene by the Cook County Sheriff's Office and temporarily closed to the public. The court-assigned receiver managing the cemetery had hoped to reopen it in September, but on October 13, 2009 visiting families found the cemetery still closed, with no statement on when it would reopen. The sheriff's office set up a searchable database with photographs of most headstones. The cemetery records were in great disarray, but the usable ones were computerized and turned over to the receiver for integration into the database.

A study of the records indicated that between 140,190 and 147,568 people were buried at Burr Oak. However, the cemetery has space for a maximum of 130,000 graves, and some areas appear never to have been used for burials. After burials resumed in November 2009, some human remains were found in areas that no one knew had been used.

As of July 2010, the cemetery was being sold to two local businessmen. The four defendants in the desecration case were free on bond and awaiting trial.

Notable burials

- Noble Drew Ali (1886-1929), prophet and founder of the Moorish Science Temple of America
- James Kokomo Arnold (1901-1968), blues musician
- Walter Barnes, bandleader who perished with 10 members of his band in the Rhythm Night Club Fire
- Lexie Bigham (1968-1995), actor
- Ezzard Charles (1921-1975), world heavyweight boxing champion
- George "Sonny" Cohn (1925-2006), jazz trumpeter with Count Basie for 30 years
- Jimmie Crutchfield (1910-1993), All-Star Negro League baseball player
- Willie Dixon (1915-1992), blues musician and songwriter
- John Donaldson (1892-1970), star pre-Negro League baseball pitcher and barnstormer businessman
- Jodie Edwards (1895-1967), of comedy duo Butterbeans and Susie
- Carl Augustus Hansberry (1895-1946), businessman and political activist, father of playwright Lorraine Hansberry
- Joseph Preston "Pete" Hill (1880-1951), Negro league baseball player elected to the Hall of Fame in 2006
- Edward Giles Irvin, founder of Kappa Alpha Psi Fraternity, Inc.
- Inman Jackson (1907-1973), player with the Harlem Globetrotters
- Roberta Martin (1907-1969), gospel music singer, pianist, composer and founder of The Roberta Martin Singers
- Graham T. Perry (1900-1960), one of the first African-Americans to serve as assistant attorney general for the State of Illinois, father of director Shauneille Perry and uncle of playwright Lorraine Hansberry
- Otis Spann (1930-1970), blues pianist
- James A. "Candy Jim" Taylor (1884-1948), Negro League baseball player and manager

- Emmett Till (1941-1955), murder victim whose death helped galvanize the U.S. Civil Rights Movement
- Ted "Highpockets" Trent (-1944), Negro League pitcher with 45 wins and 13 losses
- Bishop William M. Roberts (1876-1954), oversaw churches in Illinois, Indiana, Kentucky, Iowa, Arkansas, Minnesota, Nebraska, and Wisconsin
- Dinah Washington (1924-1963), "Queen of the Blues"
- J. Mayo Williams (1894-1980) Early blues and jazz record producer and one of the first black players in the NFL

See also

- List of United States cemeteries

External links

- Burr Oaks Cemetery – information site maintained by the Cook County Sheriff's Office [1]

Geographical coordinates: 41°39′44″N 87°43′45″W

Cultural Impact

International Boxing Hall of Fame

Geographical coordinates: 43°5.3′N 75°45.05′W

The modern **International Boxing Hall of Fame (IBHOF)** is located in Canastota, New York, United States, within driving distance from the Baseball Hall of Fame and Museum in Cooperstown and the National Soccer Hall of Fame in Oneonta. The IBHOF is one of two recognizedWikipedia:Avoid weasel words international boxing halls of fame, with the other being the World Boxing Hall of Fame.

The first Boxing Hall of Fame was sponsored by *Ring* magazine and located for decades at the offices of the Madison Square Garden in New York City. However, in 1990, as a consequence of an initiative by Ed Brophy to honor Canastota's world boxing champions, Carmen Basilio and Basilio's nephew, Billy Backus, the village of Canastota inaugurated the new museum, which showcases boxing's rich history. Multi-award winning artist Richard T. Slone was named their official artist of the International Boxing Hall of Fame in 1997 and remains so to this day.

There are ceremonies conducted every year to honor the inductees and the ceremonies are attended by many former world boxing champions, boxing celebrities and Hollywood celebrities each year.

Professional boxers have to wait five years after retirement to be eligible for election into the Hall of Fame.

On December 8, 2009, the Hall of Fame announced its Class of 2010. Living inductees include light flyweight champion Jung-Koo Chang (South Korea), featherweight champion Danny Lopez (USA), manager Shelly Finkel (USA), referee / commissioner Larry Hazzard (USA), promoter Wilfried Sauerland (Germany), matchmaker Bruce Trampler (USA) and journalist Ed Schuyler (USA). Posthumous honorees are: light heavyweight champion Lloyd Marshall (USA) in the Modern Category, featherweight champion Young Corbett II (USA), lightweight champion Rocky Kansas (USA), and light heavyweight and heavyweight contender Billy Miske (USA) in the Old-Timer Category; broadcaster Howard Cosell (USA) in the Observer Category; and Paddington Tom Jones (USA) in the Pioneer Category.

Inductees

* Year of induction in brackets

Modern era

- Muhammad Ali (1990)
- Sammy Angott (1998)
- Fred Apostoli (2003)
- Alexis Argüello (1992)
- Henry Armstrong (1990)
- Carmen Basilio (1990)
- Wilfred Benítez (1994)
- Nino Benvenuti (1996)
- Jackie Kid Berg (1992)
- Jimmy Bivins (1999)
- Joe Brown (1996)
- Ken Buchanan (2000)
- Charley Burley (1992)
- Miguel Canto (1998)
- Orlando Canizales (2009)
- Michael Carbajal (2006)
- Jimmy Carter (2000)
- Marcel Cerdan (1991)
- Antonio Cervantes (1998)
- Bobby Chacon (2005)
- Jeff Chandler (2000)
- Jung-Koo Chang (2010)
- Ezzard Charles (1990)
- Curtis Cokes (2003)
- Billy Conn (1990)
- Pipino Cuevas (2002)
- Roberto Durán (2007)
- Flash Elorde (1993)
- Jeff Fenech (2002)
- George Foreman (2003)
- Bob Foster (1990)
- Joe Frazier (1990)
- Gene Fullmer (1991)

- Khaosai Galaxy (1999)
- Víctor Galíndez (2002)
- Kid Gavilán (1990)
- Joey Giardello (1993)
- Wilfredo Gómez (1995)
- Humberto González (2006)
- Billy Graham (1992)
- Rocky Graziano (1991)
- Emile Griffith (1990)
- Marvelous Marvin Hagler (1993)
- Fighting Harada (1995)
- Larry Holmes (2008)
- Beau Jack (1991)
- Lew Jenkins (1999)
- Eder Jofre (1992)
- Ingemar Johansson (2002)
- Harold Johnson (1993)
- Ismael Laguna (2001)
- Jake LaMotta (1990)
- Sugar Ray Leonard (1997)
- Lennox Lewis (2009)
- Sonny Liston (1991)
- Nicolino Locche (2003)
- Duilio Loi (2005)
- Danny Lopez (2010)
- Ricardo Lopez (2007)
- Joe Louis (1990)
- Rocky Marciano (1990)
- Lloyd Marshall (2010)
- Joey Maxim (1994)
- Mike McCallum (2003)
- Barry McGuigan (2005)
- Brian Mitchell (2009)
- Bob Montgomery (1995)
- Carlos Monzón (1990)
- Archie Moore (1990)
- Matthew Saad Muhammad (1998)
- José Nápoles (1990)

- Azumah Nelson (2004)
- Terry Norris (2005)
- Ken Norton (1992)
- Rubén Olivares (1991)
- Bobo Olson (2000)
- Carlos Ortiz (1991)
- Manuel Ortiz (1996)
- Carlos Palomino (2004)
- László Papp (2001)
- Willie Pastrano (2001)
- Floyd Patterson (1991)
- Eusebio Pedroza (1999)
- Willie Pep (1990)

- Pascual Pérez (1995)
- Eddie Perkins (2008)
- Aaron Pryor (1996)
- Dwight Muhammad Qawi (2004)
- Sugar Ramos (2001)
- Luis Rodriguez (1997)
- Sugar Ray Robinson (1990)
- Edwin Rosario (2006)
- Sandy Saddler (1990)
- Vicente Saldivar (1999)
- Salvador Sánchez (1991)
- Max Schmeling (1992)
- Michael Spinks (1994)
- Dick Tiger (1991)
- José Torres (1997)
- Randy Turpin (2001)
- Jersey Joe Walcott (1990)
- Pernell Whitaker (2007)
- Holman Williams (2008)
- Ike Williams (1990)
- Chalky Wright (1997)
- Tony Zale (1991)
- Daniel Zaragoza (2004)
- Carlos Zárate (1994)
- Fritzie Zivic (1993)

Old Timers

- Lou Ambers (1992)
- Baby Arizmendi (2004)
- Abe Attell (1990)
- Max Baer (1995)
- Jimmy Barry (2000)
- Benny Bass (2002)
- Battling Battalino (2003)
- Paul Berlenbach (2001)
- James J. Braddock (2001)
- Jack Britton (1990)
- Lou Brouillard (2006)
- Panama Al Brown (1992)
- Tommy Burns (1996)
- Tony Canzoneri (1990)
- Georges Carpentier (1991)
- Kid Chocolate (1994)
- Joe Choynski (1998)
- James J. Corbett (1990)
- Young Corbett II (2010)
- Young Corbett III (2004)
- Johnny Coulon (1999)
- Eugene Criqui (2005)
- Les Darcy (1993)
- Jack Delaney (1996)
- Jack Dempsey (1990)
- Jack (Nonpareil) Dempsey (1992)
- Jim Driscoll (1990)
- Jack Dillon (1995)

- George Dixon (1990)
- Johnny Dundee (1991)
- Sixto Escobar (2002)
- Jackie Fields (2004)
- Bob Fitzsimmons (1990)
- Tiger Flowers (1993)
- Joe Gans (1990)
- Frankie Genaro (1998)

- Mike Gibbons (1992)
- Tommy Gibbons (1993)
- George Godfrey (2007)
- Harry Greb (1990)
- Young Griffo (1991)
- Harry Harris (2002)
- Len Harvey (2008)
- Pete Herman (1997)
- Peter Jackson (1990)
- Joe Jeanette (1997)
- James J. Jeffries (1990)
- Jack Johnson (1990)
- Gorilla Jones (2009)
- Rocky Kansas (2010)
- Louis "Kid" Kaplan (2003)
- Stanley Ketchel (1990)
- Dixie Kid (2002)
- Johnny Kilbane (1995)
- Frank Klaus (2008)
- Fidel LaBarba (1996)
- Sam Langford (1990)
- George "Kid" Lavigne (1998)
- Benny Leonard (1990)
- Battling Levinsky (2000)
- Harry Lewis (2008)
- John Henry Lewis (1994)
- Ted "Kid" Lewis (1992)
- Tommy Loughran (1991)
- Benny Lynch (1998)
- Joe Lynch (2005)
- Sammy Mandell (1998)
- Jack McAuliffe (1995)
- Charles "Kid" McCoy (1991)
- Packey McFarland (1992)
- Terry McGovern (1990)
- Jimmy McLarnin (1991)
- Sam McVey (1999)
- Freddie Miller (1997)

- Billy Miske (2010)
- Charley Mitchell (2002)
- Pedro Montañez (2007)
- Owen Moran (2002)
- Kid Norfolk (2007)
- Battling Nelson (1992)
- Philadelphia Jack O'Brien (1994)
- Billy Papke (2001)
- Billy Petrolle (2000)
- Willie Ritchie (2004)

- Maxie Rosenbloom (1993)
- Barney Ross (1990)
- Tommy Ryan (1991)
- Jack Sharkey (1994)
- Jimmy Slattery (2006)
- Tom Sharkey (2003)
- Mysterious Billy Smith (2009)
- Billy Soose (2009)
- Freddie Steele (1999)
- Young Stribling (1996)
- Charles "Bud" Taylor (2005)
- Lew Tendler (1999)
- Marcel Thil (2005)
- Gene Tunney (1990)
- Pancho Villa (1994)
- Barbados Joe Walcott (1991)
- Mickey Walker (1990)
- Freddie Welsh (1997)
- Jimmy Wilde (1990)
- Jess Willard (2003)
- Kid Williams (1996)
- Harry Wills (1992)
- Ad Wolgast (2000)
- Midget Wolgast (2001)
- Teddy Yarosz (2006)

Pioneers

- Barney Aaron (2001)
- Young Barney Aaron (2007)
- Caleb Baldwin (2003)
- Jem Belcher (1992)
- Benjamin Brain (1994)
- Jack Broughton (1990)
- James Burke (1992)
- Jem Carney (2006)
- Arthur Chambers (2000)
- Tom Cribb (1991)
- Dick Curtis (2007)
- Dan Donnelly (2008)
- Professor Mike Donovan (1998)
- Paddy Duffy (1994)
- Billy Edwards (2004)
- James Figg (1992)
- Joe Goss (2003)
- John C. Heenan (2002)
- Tom Hyer (2009)
- John Jackson (1992)
- Tom Johnson (1995)
- Paddington Tom Jones (2010)
- Tom King (1992)
- Nat Langham (1992)
- Jem Mace (1990)
- Daniel Mendoza (1990)
- Tom Molineaux (1997)
- John Morrissey (1996)
- Henry Pearce (1993)
- Jack Randall (2005)
- Bill Richmond (1999)
- Dutch Sam (1997)
- Young Dutch Sam (2002)
- Tom Sayers (1990)
- Tom Spring (1992)
- John L. Sullivan (1990)
- Bendigo Thompson (1991)
- Jem Ward (1995)

Non-participants

- Thomas S. Andrews (1992)
- Ray Arcel (1991)
- Bob Arum (1999)
- Jarvis Astaire (2006)
- Giuseppe Ballarati (1999)
- George Benton (2001)
- Whitey Bimstein (2006)
- Jack Blackburn (1992)
- William A. Brady (1998)
- Umberto Branchini (2004)
- Teddy Brenner (1993)
- Amilcar Brusa (2007)
- Bill Cayton (2005)
- John Graham Chambers (1990)
- Don Chargin (2001)
- Stanley Christodoulou (2004)
- Gil Clancy (1993)
- Irving Cohen (2002)
- James W. Coffroth (1991)
- Cuco Conde (2007)
- Cus D'Amato (1995)
- Jeff Dickson (2000)
- Arthur Donovan (1993)
- Mickey Duff (1999)
- Angelo Dundee (1994)
- Chris Dundee (1994)
- Don Dunphy (1993)
- Dan Duva (2003)
- Lou Duva (1998)
- Aileen Eaton (2002)
- Pierce Egan (1991)
- Shelly Finkel (2010)
- Nat Fleischer (1990)
- Richard Kyle Fox (1997)
- Dewey Fragetta (2003)
- Don Fraser (2005)
- Eddie Futch (1994)
- Billy Gibson (2009)
- Charley Goldman (1992)
- Ruby Goldstein (1994)
- Bob Goodman (2009)
- Murray Goodman (1999)
- Bill Gore (2008)
- Abe J. Greene (2009)
- Larry Hazzard (2010)
- Akihiko Honda (2009)
- Joe Humphreys (1997)
- Sam Ichinose (2001)
- Jimmy Jacobs (1993)
- Mike Jacobs (1990)
- Jimmy Johnston (1999)
- Jack Kearns (1990)
- Don King (1997)
- Tito Lectoure (1997)
- A.J. Liebling (1992)
- Hugh, Earl of Lonsdale (1996)
- Harry Markson (1992)
- John, Marquess of Queensberry (1990)
- Arthur Mercante (1995)
- Dan Morgan (2000)
- William Muldoon (1996)
- Gilbert Odd (1995)
- Tom O'Rourke (1999)
- Mogens Palle (2008)
- Dan Parker (1996)
- George Parnassus (1991)
- J Russell Peltz (2004)
- Tex Rickard (1990)
- Irving Rudd (1999)
- Rodolfo Sabbatini (2006)
- Lope Sarreal (2005)
- Wilfried Sauerland (2010)
- George Siler (1995)
- Sam Silverman (2002)
- Jack Solomons (1995)
- Emanuel Steward (1997)
- José Sulaimán (2007)
- Sam Taub (1995)
- Herman Taylor (1998)
- Bruce Trampler (2010)
- Lou Viscusi (2004)
- Jimmy Walker (1992)
- Frank Warren (2008)
- Al Weill (2003)

Observers

- Dave Anderson (2008)
- Lester Bromberg (2001)
- Jimmy Cannon (2002)
- Ralph Citro (2001)
- Howard Cosell (2010)
- Tad Dorgan (2007)

- Jack Fiske (2003)
- Paul Gallico (2009)
- Bill Gallo (2001)
- Reg Gutteridge (2002)
- W.C. Heinz (2004)
- Jersey Jones (2005)

- Hank Kaplan (2006)
- Joe Koizumi (2008)
- Hugh McIlvanney (2009)
- Larry Merchant (2009)
- Harry Mullan (2005)
- Barney Nagler (2004)

- LeRoy Neiman (2007)
- Damon Runyon (2002)
- Budd Schulberg (2003)
- Ed Schuyler (2010)
- Bert Sugar (2005)
- Stanley Weston (2006)

External links

- IBHOF [1] official website

Article Sources and Contributors

Ezzard Charles *Source*: http://en.wikipedia.org/?oldid=388124268 *Contributors*:

Ken Overlin *Source*: http://en.wikipedia.org/?oldid=389186395 *Contributors*:

Teddy Yarosz *Source*: http://en.wikipedia.org/?oldid=389214022 *Contributors*:

Charley Burley *Source*: http://en.wikipedia.org/?oldid=383772391 *Contributors*:

Archie Moore *Source*: http://en.wikipedia.org/?oldid=385811696 *Contributors*: Kumioko

Jimmy Bivins *Source*: http://en.wikipedia.org/?oldid=389799273 *Contributors*:

Lloyd Marshall *Source*: http://en.wikipedia.org/?oldid=338292067 *Contributors*: BD2412

Joe Baksi *Source*: http://en.wikipedia.org/?oldid=334546094 *Contributors*:

Jersey Joe Walcott *Source*: http://en.wikipedia.org/?oldid=389988116 *Contributors*: Fep70

Joe Louis *Source*: http://en.wikipedia.org/?oldid=390448320 *Contributors*: Andrwsc

Joey Maxim *Source*: http://en.wikipedia.org/?oldid=384393100 *Contributors*: Bender235

Rex Layne *Source*: http://en.wikipedia.org/?oldid=390596393 *Contributors*:

Coley Wallace *Source*: http://en.wikipedia.org/?oldid=390529671 *Contributors*:

Bob Satterfield *Source*: http://en.wikipedia.org/?oldid=390179770 *Contributors*: 1 anonymous edits

Rocky Marciano *Source*: http://en.wikipedia.org/?oldid=389755139 *Contributors*: Fep70

The distance (boxing) *Source*: http://en.wikipedia.org/?oldid=388237174 *Contributors*: Troglo

Middleweight *Source*: http://en.wikipedia.org/?oldid=389417552 *Contributors*: 1 anonymous edits

Chicago Golden Gloves *Source*: http://en.wikipedia.org/?oldid=287253330 *Contributors*: Vl'hurg

World Boxing Association *Source*: http://en.wikipedia.org/?oldid=389604718 *Contributors*: 1 anonymous edits

Heavyweight *Source*: http://en.wikipedia.org/?oldid=388338177 *Contributors*: 1 anonymous edits

Light heavyweight *Source*: http://en.wikipedia.org/?oldid=386102186 *Contributors*: 1 anonymous edits

List of heavyweight boxing champions *Source*: http://en.wikipedia.org/?oldid=389917251 *Contributors*: 1 anonymous edits

Lawrenceville, Georgia *Source*: http://en.wikipedia.org/?oldid=390079288 *Contributors*:

African American *Source*: http://en.wikipedia.org/?oldid=390324902 *Contributors*: Therock40756

Woodward High School *Source*: http://en.wikipedia.org/?oldid=341053616 *Contributors*: Mandarax

Orthodox stance *Source*: http://en.wikipedia.org/?oldid=390559010 *Contributors*: TeleComNasSprVen

Double bass *Source*: http://en.wikipedia.org/?oldid=389371949 *Contributors*:

Burr Oak Cemetery *Source*: http://en.wikipedia.org/?oldid=387687151 *Contributors*: Igbo

International Boxing Hall of Fame *Source*: http://en.wikipedia.org/?oldid=389930517 *Contributors*: 1 anonymous edits

CPSIA information can be obtained at www.ICGtesting.com
Printed in the USA
LVOW111923150413

329247LV00019B/1000/P

9 781276 188494